The Folded Paper

Inventing Cyberdiplomacy

SIOBHAN MacDERMOTT

ISBN-13: 978-1985886742

To Mom and Dad for all the dining room diplomacy, and to Aodhan for
making my world complete.

TABLE OF CONTENTS

FOREWORD

Admiral James G. Stavridis (Ret.)

Few words have fallen so far so fast in recent years—in recent months, even—than *diplomacy* and *diplomat.* In fact, I can think of only two that have arguably toppled farther and faster: *politics* and *politician.* The precipitous decline of all these terms is more than a linguistic phenomenon. It is a symptom of a national and international malaise, a cataclysm of collective cynicism that is deadly dangerous for the United States and for every other nation on the planet. These days, public service—encompassing the professions of politician and bureaucrat (another good word that has become a slur) as well as diplomat—is often treated with a mixture of suspicion, contempt, and derision, not just by the public but by national leaders and the politicians, bureaucrats, and diplomats themselves.

Skillful diplomacy, like sincere political debate, is often dismissed out of hand as weakness, especially by presidents and prime ministers who make a great show of embracing their military. As a proud career naval officer who became a proud student of diplomacy and the dean of graduate school of diplomacy and global law, I can assure you that no matter how much a president may scoff at diplomacy, the generals and the admirals invariably look upon it as both the preferred alternative to war and a force multiplier of military readiness, military presence, and military action. Concerning the hard work of preparing for battle, General George S. Patton liked to say that a "pint of sweat saves a gallon of blood." Substitute *diplomacy* for *sweat,* and I'll endorse the sentiment. Today, the one group of public servants from which you hear no disparagement of diplomacy are officers and enlisted personnel of the United States Navy, Army, Air Force, and Marines.

Still, the identity crisis that currently grips diplomacy and diplomats is real, acute, and not entirely inflicted from outside of the profession. No public calling is more venerable than diplomacy, as evidenced by the so-called Armana letters—clay tablets recording diplomatic correspondence between the Egyptian administration of the Eighteenth Dynasty (1550-1292 BC) and the kingdom's ambassadors in Canaan and Amurru. Yet, deeply rooted as it is, no public service has responded more haltingly than diplomacy has to the rapid evolution of modern digital technology. If non-diplomats—including politicians and the public—often perceive diplomats as circumspect, aloof, legalistic, mired in ceremony, and theoretical rather than practical, it is because the role of the diplomat has lost much of the definition it had in the days before the proliferation of mass communication. Moreover, as mass communication ("traditional" broadcast communication) has itself been eclipsed by digital communication (interactive communication on the Internet), the definition of the diplomat's role has become even more obscure and, seemingly, more remote from day-to-day politics and from the day-to-day concerns of most private citizens. It is as if the world, made smaller by the global Internet, has failed to leave sufficient room for diplomacy, at least as diplomacy was practiced from ancient times through the twentieth century.

Siobhan MacDermott leads the Global Cyber Public Policy team for the multinational Bank of America. She combines an educational background in liberal arts (B.A. in German language and literature, Temple University), management (Thunderbird School of Global Management), and a Global Master of Arts in Law and Diplomacy (Fletcher School at Tufts University). She has worked in eight countries and speaks five languages. To *The Folded Paper: Inventing Cyberdiplomacy,* she brings an advanced academic background in diplomacy as well as practical experience in international business, technology, cyber security, and public policy. This multifaceted perspective informs the outlook of a book that seeks to open up diplomacy to both the challenges and the opportunities of our intensively interconnected world. It stakes out the vision of someone who both understands and respects diplomacy as essential to the enlightened co-prosperity, let alone survival, of nations, but who is also anxious to coax diplomatic art and science, theory and practice into an age in which digital networks will only continue to weave themselves more thoroughly and intricately into the fabric of government as well as governance, of global politics, global commerce, and, yes, global conflict. You are about to read a book that proves one can be realistic about the prospects for diplomacy in our time without relinquishing optimism for the cold embrace of cynicism.

James Stavridis is a retired U.S. Navy admiral and former Supreme Allied Commander at NATO for four years, He is currently dean of the Fletcher School of Law and Diplomacy at Tufts University, a graduate school for international affairs.

PREFACE

During the third quarter of 2017, according to the U.S. Census Bureau, retail e-commerce sales totaled $115.3 billion, an increase of 3.6 percent (±0.7%) from the second quarter of 2017. The third quarter 2017 e-commerce estimate increased 15.5 percent (±1.1%) from the third quarter of 2016 while total retail sales increased 4.3 percent (±0.4%) in the same period. E-commerce sales in the third quarter of 2017 accounted for 9.1 percent of total sales. Total retail sales for the third quarter of 2017, brick and mortar plus e-commerce were estimated at $1,268.9 billion, an increase of just 1.1 percent (±0.2%) from the second quarter of 2017.[1] The migration of commerce to the Internet continues. As *Forbes* observed at the end of 2012, "The smart brick-and-mortar players, ... are adapting to the new realities. Take Macy's: The 154-year-old retail chain saw online sales rise 40% in 2011 while same-store sales grew just 5.3%. The company is transforming nearly 300 of its stores into distribution centers to speed up shipping for online consumers."[2] If (to paraphrase Mark Twain) reports of the death of brick-and-mortar retailers were "greatly exaggerated" in 2012, the exaggeration was even greater in 2017 as even more brick-and-mortar enterprises were finding ways to migrate to e-commerce without knocking down all those bricks.[3]

More and more governments are taking a digital leaf from the e-book of e-commerce and are making earnest efforts to engage their citizens online. A few governments, such as that of Estonia—popularly known as "e-Stonia," because of its early and thorough embrace of the Internet—have been way ahead of the curve. That country votes online, its legislative bodies meet online, and most routine government business is conducted online. Other governments, like that of the United States, have experienced notable failures to use the Internet effectively, as in the infamous rollout of the Affordable Care Act late in 2013. Nevertheless, a 2017 article in *Forbes* enumerated "Top 6 Digital Transformation Trends in Government."[4] These included the proliferation of the Internet of things (IoT) to create smart cities through the use of "built-in sensors in cars, street lights, traffic cameras and electricity grids" that continually collect information and process it to regulate everything from traffic signals to power loads; automation to replace certain workers; advanced cybersecurity; use of mobile technology to do business with government agencies; and extensive data collection and analytics. For most citizens, however, the most visible digital transformation is the growing migration of government agencies to online platforms, especially for services involving the payment of fees (such as DMV licenses and tags).

That national governments will, like "the smart brick-and-mortar" merchants, have no choice but to conduct more and more of their activities in cyberspace is therefore hardly a prognostication worthy of Nostradamus. It is happening now. The bolder and far more consequential move from physical space to cyberspace will come not on the national level but in the international arena. The Internet has made borders and boundaries permeable—although, as we will see, hardly to the extent that some Internet visionaries either now claim or foresee. Unquestionably, the Internet has tended to transform hierarchical and centralized power structures into networks of peer-to-peer interactivity, as was dramatically demonstrated (for example) in the Arab Awakening ("Arab Spring") that began in 2010. What has already taken place as the transformation of brick-and-mortar commerce into e-commerce is both preview of and prelude to an era in which some aspects of traditional diplomacy will be augmented, complemented, and even supplanted by cyberdiplomacy. In the notable and notorious instances of "Russian meddling" (a phrase that has become something of term of art) in U.S., French, and German elections, digital platforms and the Internet have been used to covertly influence the outcome of elections and perhaps even to alter actual vote tallies.[5]

As with the slow but steady shift from brick-and-mortar shopping to online commerce, the adoption of cyberdiplomacy will involve both technological as well as cultural transformation. I believe it will also draw on another technological and cultural innovation that has been both enabled and driven by the ascendency of the Internet. This is the open source movement, which is having a profound effect on the way software is developed, distributed, and continuously improved.

This book is about the transformation, both ongoing and coming, with all its promise and threat. It is a vision, a plan, and a call to action. It is about becoming a "smart player" on the global stage and catching up to a technology already proliferating. It is about mastering that technology technically, politically, and morally to reinvent diplomacy for a hyperconnected world. It is about cyberdiplomacy.

3

INTRODUCTION
THE FOLDED PAPER

"War," the early nineteenth-century military theorist Carl von Clausewitz wrote, "is . . . a true political instrument, a continuation of political intercourse carried on with other means."[6] By this definition, war is the very opposite of diplomacy. In fact, if we wanted to convey a basic definition of *diplomacy,* we could simply say that it is the resolution of international "political intercourse" without war and that war, conversely, is the "other means" of conducting such intercourse. Diplomacy is used if nations do not wish to resort to war, and war is what happens if they do not choose diplomacy or if diplomacy fails.

If the preceding paragraph had been written—and was also being read—at the very end of the twentieth century or earlier, the absolute opposition of war and diplomacy would be an entirely adequate beginning to understanding the nature of both war and diplomacy. Today, however, with the Internet having so thoroughly established cyberspace as a dimension of human activity as real and legitimate as time and space, it is no longer sufficient to propose war as *the* definitive and defining antithesis of diplomacy.

Consider: During the week of April 27, 2007, a succession of massive distributed denial of service (DDoS) attacks (which transform multiple computers into "zombies" by infecting them with malware, commandeering them to flood the bandwidth or resources of the targeted system so that new connections cannot be accepted) paralyzed Estonia.[7] This formerly Soviet-occupied, now-independent, republic was (and remains) one of the world's most networked nations. Since late 2005, the Estonian government has conducted most of its operations exclusively on the Internet, Estonians vote online, Cabinet-level meetings are held online, and the majority of the Estonian people access their bank accounts online—exclusively. All of this, operations basic to the routine conduct of Estonian life, ground to a halt, beginning on April 27, 2007.

It was on this very day that the Estonian government announced its decision to move a Soviet-installed World War II monument known as "The Bronze Soldier of Tallinn," along with the buried remains of some Red Army soldiers, from a plot in Tallinn's central park to the Defense Forces Cemetery located outside the city. Estonia had declared independence from the disintegrating Soviet Union on August 20, 1991. Sixteen years later, ethnic Estonians—most of the country's population—were pleased to see an unhappy memory of the oppressive Soviet occupation moved outside of the capital. Members of the country's Russian minority, however, protested the move and even rioted. What the majority regarded as a hateful artifact, they saw as a sacred memorial to World War II Soviet heroism.

The disorder in physical space was quickly succeeded in cyberspace by the DDoS attacks. Some of these came from individuals using such low-tech methods as ping floods (the attacker sending multiple "ping" packets at high speed without waiting for reply), but others were executed by international botnets that are typically used to broadcast spam. Individuals do not mount botnet assaults, which require the kind of investment associated with big business or governments. Even as the DDoS attacks multiplied, Russian chat rooms hummed with calls for patriotic Russian Internet users to join in on the attacks. The chat rooms posted complete how-to instructions.

U.S. researchers later reported that, at the height of the attacks, Estonian government websites built to handle a thousand visits a day received 2,000 every second. A network intended to handle 2 million megabits of traffic per second was flooded with some 200 million. During one sustained assault of about ten hours, more than 90 million megabits per second of data were directed against the websites of the Ministries of Foreign Affairs and Justice, which were throttled into a total shut down. The Estonian Reform Party website was defaced with digital graffiti that included a Hitler-esque cookie-duster moustache scrawled across the face of Prime Minister Andrus Ansip. On May 3, the DDoS assault was directed against the Estonian private sector, forcing most of the country's banks to shut down. On May 9, the Russian anniversary of the end of World War II, the attacks reached the point of greatest intensity. By this time, however, the Estonian government had managed to quadruple the data capacity of its systems, and the effect of the onslaught began to diminish.

Throughout the cyber siege of Estonia, official Moscow stubbornly denied involvement. Yet the DDoS attacks were of such massive scope (at times involving up to 100,000 "zombie" PCs) and duration that international experts were unanimous in their judgment that state support was a certainty. Nevertheless, hard evidence conclusively connecting the Russian government to the cyberattacks has yet to emerge, but one Konstantin Goloskokov, a leading member of a pro-Kremlin Russian youth organization called Nashi, admitted that Nashi had been involved. Goloskokov was not only a Nashi activist, he was also assistant to Sergei Markov, a Duma Deputy (the equivalent of a U.S. member of Congress). Nashi—its name is short for an organization known in full as the "Youth Democratic Anti-Fascist Movement 'NASHI'"—was officially funded by private Russian business interests but nevertheless endorsed upon its April 15, 2005 creation by the Russian government. Today, it continues to receive the enthusiastic endorsement of prominent government figures, including Vladislav Surkov, in 2007 first deputy chief of the presidential staff, and since December 2011 deputy prime minister. Nashi was implicated not only in the cyberattacks against Estonia, but also in internal Russian government operations against certain "banned" political parties and organizations.

The 2007 cyberattacks against Estonia were not acts of diplomacy, at least not as diplomacy is conventionally understood. But were they acts of war? Not exactly, at least not as warfare is conventionally understood. The battlefield never went "kinetic." No bombs were detonated. No guns were fired. If anything, the 2007 cyberattacks were both diplomacy (politics) *and* war carried out "with other means."

The 2007 cyber assault on Estonia, the cyber component of the Russia-Georgia War of 2008, and the DDoS attacks against Krygyzstan in 2009 (launched after that former Soviet republic granted the United States permission to build an air force base in its Manas District) demonstrate that the Internet has rendered obsolescent certain assumptions and practices of both conventional diplomacy and its conventional antithesis, kinetic—that is, shooting—war.

Now consider a more recent event. In 2012, a series of ads was published on www.arcticready.com, a website that appeared to belong to the Shell Oil Company. The ads, however, featured such messages as ludicrous appeals for charitable donations to the multibillion-dollar company and, under the headline "LET'S HIT THE BEACH," a picture of Shell's *Noble Discoverer* offshore drilling rig, which made headlines when it lost its moorings in Alaska's Dutch Harbor in July 2012. In fact, the website and the ads were parts of an extraordinarily elaborate hoax created by Greenpeace to stir opposition to Shell's plans for Arctic drilling. In addition to the online ads, the hoax campaign included a

Twitter feed, YouTube videos that went viral, and even an interactive game.[8]

In the past, Greenpeace protestors physically harassed or even invaded oil rigs. What *Forbes* called a "social media nightmare," which commanded more popular and media attention than many actual disasters do, was created without anyone leaving shore.[9] As Witold Henisz, a professor of management at the Wharton School, observed, "Today, thanks to the Internet and the spread of social media, anyone with a smart phone and a grudge can push a negative message out to a global audience within a matter of seconds. Activists are increasingly able to access virtually everything companies or their suppliers do anywhere in the world. The financial and reputational damage a single individual or small group is capable of causing can be catastrophic."[10]

To be sure, neither Greenpeace (an NGO) nor Shell (a multinational corporation) is a nation, but substitute "Country A" for *Greenpeace* and "Country B" for *Shell*, and you have a picture of what "political intercourse carried on with other means" could look like when "carried on" in cyberspace rather than physical space. As the U.S., French, and German elections of 2016 revealed, the Russian government, through a body known as the Internet Research Agency(IRA) and other so-called troll farms creates and disseminates fake news via major social networks, online newspaper sites, and video hosting services (such as YouTube) to promote the Kremlin's interests in (among other things) foreign relations by attempting to influence the elections of other nations.[11]

For all practical purposes, perception readily becomes reality online, and a diplomacy designed in and for the old offline world is simply inadequate to cope. Diplomacy is in need of reinvention for our hyperconnected planet.

The subtitle of this book is *Inventing Cyberdiplomacy*. This requires *reinventing* traditional diplomacy—which emphatically does not mean scrapping it as a thing without value. On the contrary, I believe that reinventing diplomacy as cyberdiplomacy requires, as a first step, returning to the very roots of diplomacy.

We can take that step right now. The English word *diplomacy* comes most immediately from the French *diplomatie,* which, in turn, derives from the Latin *diploma,* meaning "a letter of recommendation or authority." In this sense, a *diplomat,* the official charged with practicing diplomacy, is the holder of a letter of recommendation or authority. But we are interested in roots, so we must go back from Latin to Greek, where we find *diplōma* (δίπλωμα), meaning a "folded paper," or, more specifically, a "paper folded in two."

A letter—including a letter of authority—can be folded and, in fact, usually is. But I suggest we think of the folded paper at the root of diplomacy not literally or narrowly as the diplomat's credential document, but as whatever substantive message the diplomat carries. Folding the sheet hides the content, yet the document can be readily unfolded and the message revealed. The folded paper is a metaphor for both secrecy *and* revelation. The message is secret until delivered. This makes it confidential rather than deceptive—in the end, transparent rather than opaque. What is more, a "paper folded in two" suggests a pair of equal halves. On one half, the diplomat may deliver his or her message. On the other half, the diplomat's counterpart may inscribe his or her response. The metaphor here is of secrecy and revelation plus the exchange of message and response, with all four elements given equal weight, equal value. It is a metaphor that expresses the essence of diplomacy. It is the ideal to which classical or traditional diplomacy aspires—or should.

The question we must answer is whether cyberdiplomacy— diplomacy reinvented for a digitally interconnected world—moves us closer to or further from realizing the ideal and achieving the aspiration. As the examples of cyber aggression from sources as different as Russia and Greenpeace demonstrate, our intensive connectivity renders us vulnerable to acts ranging from cross-border intimidation, vandalism, and terrorism to distortion and reputation bashing. On the other hand, the use of mobile platforms, social media, and the Internet in general has sometimes overcome the efforts of governments and tyrants to suppress popular movements toward democracy. The Arab Spring (more accurately called the Arab Awakening) is a case in point. The Internet has had perhaps its most immediately dramatic effect on the conduct of "hearts and minds diplomacy" or "public diplomacy," diplomacy that seeks to exercise influence directly on a nation's people rather than through the official channels of government. One of those key channels, traditional diplomacy, struggles mightily simply to keep up with the speed of digitally driven public diplomacy.

Even while running so desperately, however, breathless diplomats must repeatedly ask themselves if speed, a product as well as an imperative of technology, is compatible with sound diplomatic decisions and foreign policy. The *people* demand that governments move at the speed of interconnected, interactive digital communications. But the role of good government, particularly republican (as opposed to purely democratic) government, is to *respond* to the demands of the people even while *leading* the people, which often requires moderating or even refusing their demands. At the very least, it requires deliberation, and deliberation requires time. In short, good government and good foreign policy may well be fundamentally incompatible with speed.

Nevertheless, cyberdiplomacy has arrived. We are still in a very early iteration—perhaps 1.0 for covert digital public diplomacy in the form of fake news, but somewhere between an alpha and beta release in the practice of more sophisticated, overt, reality-based diplomacy between governments rather than between governments and the people of other countries. Nevertheless, even at this early point in the digital game, we can predict much about the effect of digital technology on the conduct of diplomacy by looking at another traditional arena of organized human interchange, one with which we already have substantial Internet experience. Consider e-commerce—the transition from marketing, buying, and selling in brick-and-mortar environments to doing these things online. At its best and biggest, e-commerce removes many of the points of economic friction inherent in commerce as it is conducted in the physical world. Online, a consumer has access to virtually every product offered for sale, to every maker of a given product, to every alternative to a given product, and to every purveyor of that product. Economics 101 tells us that consumers will seek the lowest price or, perhaps, the best value in a particular product. In theory, the makers and sellers who offer the highest value—the most desirable product at the most competitive price—will win. Before the ascendency of e-commerce, however, the physical world inevitably introduced many frictions that mitigated against the efficient execution of economic theory. A consumer's choice was limited by the availability of products in that consumer's geographical area, the retail outlets conveniently available to that consumer in a given place and at a particular time, that consumer's limited knowledge of the range of products and offers available, and the merchants' very limited capability to learn what users of a particular product think of it. E-commerce has removed most of these frictions, thereby bringing the ideal of supply-and-demand economics much closer to daily realization. E-commerce makes markets far more efficient.

Part of the efficiency of e-commerce, as just implied, is the transparency it tends to create. Not only do online shoppers have the opportunity to quickly and easily find the lowest price on an item, they also instantly see alternatives to their intended target, and, typically, they can quickly learn a great deal about the item as well as the category to which it belongs. Also typically, consumers can read the opinions of current users of the item or alternatives to it. Because e-commerce gives consumers unprecedented access to information, it tends toward transparency, and it tends as well toward the realization of the free market that is at the heart of supply-and-demand economic theory.

Another dimension of e-commerce is analogous to the folded paper metaphor of diplomacy. E-commerce allows for secrecy as well as sharing. A consumer may feel inhibited in the purchase of certain items in a brick-and-mortar environment. Everything from adult diapers, to sex toys, to applying for a loan gives some people pause. Online, alone with keyboard and screen, presumably protected by a password, consumer inhibitions tend to vanish in a halo of enabling secrecy and anonymity. At the same time, the very consumers who might hesitate to purchase certain categories of merchandise in a crowded department store freely share their evaluation of those very items with potentially millions online. So there is also a degree of sharing. The paper is folded, but can be unfolded at will. Moreover, the sharing possible in e-commerce extends beyond consumers offering their experiences to one another. Merchants and makers are also eager for their digital customers to share information with them—so eager that they may track and record consumer activity online with or without the permission of the Internet user. At its best—its most positively productive—e-commerce leverages many opportunities to satisfy the individual customer by tailoring products and offers directly to him or her, based on the data he or she has already shared with the merchant or the maker. At its worst, online tracking is (and is perceived as) an unacceptable invasion of privacy, a deceptive intrusion.

As with commerce, offline or online, transaction is at the core of diplomacy, offline or online. For this reason, our experience with e-commerce—already extensive, and developing further by the nanosecond—should tell us a lot about what cyberdiplomacy will look like. Creating digital efficiencies, cyberdiplomacy will reduce or remove many of the frictions that inhibit, delay, or distort legal and diplomatic transactions in the offline world. Among the "frictions" reduced (but, we will see, certainly not removed) are national borders, the divisions set up between sectors within a society, and those that demarcate departments within a government bureaucracy. The tendency of digital technology to render walls, borders, and administrative divisions in varying degrees permeable will profoundly shape diplomacy conducted online.

The same qualities that create permeability can be expected also to promote transparency in cyberdiplomacy. Otto von Bismarck is famously—albeit mistakenly—credited with having warned, "Laws are like sausages—it is best not to see them being made." In government-to-government diplomacy conducted online, much of the sausage factory will become visible. This transparency is also likely to promote something akin to a "free market" in international relations, an exchange in which the features, pitfalls, drawbacks, benefits, and options in any set of decisions concerning cross-border relations will be more fully and completely on public display. Given greater access to the elements of diplomacy, people will have the opportunity to make themselves meaningfully heard in digitally enabled democracies that have overcome many of the frictions created when transactions are limited to the physical world. In the concluding chapter of this book, I suggest the Internet will operate on diplomacy in much the same way that it has operated on the creation of information and knowledge and even in the creation of software itself—through open source. Web applications that allow people to intensively interact and thereby collaborate with others, called "wikis," proliferate on the Internet. The most familiar and perhaps most successful of these websites is Wikipedia, an open source encyclopedia. "Open source" is a collaborative model of development that allows open—indeed, universal—access to the design, plan, or blueprint of a product for the purpose of continuous customization and improvement by those who use the product. Open source methods have become common in the collaborative creation of software (for "blueprint," substitute the term *source code*—computer instructions written in a human-readable language, rather than machine language, and therefore universally accessible). I believe open source methods will become a foundational feature of public diplomacy as cyberdiplomacy.

While cyberdiplomacy will enable as it is enabled by open source methodologies, digital technology will both enable and enhance opportunities for secrecy as well as sharing. By enabling citizens to make their needs and opinions more effectively heard, cyberdiplomacy will tend to reshape relations between governments so that these interactions will no longer be strictly between governments, but between governments *and* peoples. Cyberdiplomacy will bring democracy out of its national boundaries and into the global community. Yet, like e-commerce, cyberdiplomacy has the capability *both* to increase transparency *and* to enhance confidentiality and secrecy. Secrecy has always played a role in some aspects of diplomacy, and its selective application will always be necessary. Not without good reason, the paper the diplomat carries is folded rather than opened flat. Networked digital technology has the potential both to enhance and destroy secrecy. In addition, it invites the abuse of secrecy—its indiscriminate application to just about everything, as governments habitually confound opacity with secrecy even as they misguidedly declare secrecy incompatible with transparency. Whatever else is achieved by the application of digital technology to diplomacy, it will provide the great opportunity of a new start, the urgent incentive to reassess and rebalance the demands of general openness with those of selective secrecy. The transactions between government and government as well as between governments and citizens will move from opacity to "wide open secrecy": the paper folded, but unsealed.

CHAPTER 1
MEDIA: FROM MASS TO MASSIVE

True autocracies are rare in history. All but the most arrogant or brutally stupid monarchs recognize they have a neck and that its flesh will not fare well in an encounter with an axe. The satirist Juvenal wrote (*Satires* 10:81) that politicians may purchase votes for "bread and circuses" (*panem et circenses*), and Julius Caesar, decisive and ruthless as he was, sought popular support by staging elaborate public entertainments and erecting many lavish public works. (Even so, he was finally unable to avoid assassination.) Elizabeth I of England went beyond both coercion and bribery. She sought to understand her subjects, their wants, and their needs, by descending from her throne, leaving her palace, and literally going out among them. It was no pleasure. An overland journey in Elizabethan England was slow, tedious, filthy, and expensive. Mounting what was called a "royal progress" through the realm required no fewer than four hundred wagons, together with as many as 2,400 pack horses, which moved along at a rate of perhaps twelve miles a day—on a very good day. The services of about a thousand people were needed to manage all of this, and Elizabeth did it just about every summer of her long reign. "We come," she explained to the people of one town she visited, "for the hearts and allegiance of our subjects."[12]

Inconvenient, expensive, and even dangerous as it was, the queen believed there was no better way to understand her subjects and to communicate her affection, regard, and care for them. To assess the state of the kingdom, there was no better way than by direct contact with it, and no more effective means of building the loyalty of her subjects. At least, not prior to a technological era in which timely and detailed remote communication was possible.

Public diplomacy before real-time media technology

The idea of people-to-people government is not new, and the notion of people-to-people diplomacy—so-called public diplomacy—is an extension of it. The development of mass media influenced and ultimately transformed the conduct of both people-to-people government and public diplomacy. Thomas Jefferson famously communicated to fellow Virginian Edward Carrington his extreme advocacy of journalistically mediated people-to-people government, writing in 1787 that because the "basis of our governments being the opinion of the people, the very first object should be to keep that right; and were it left to me to decide whether we should have a government without newspapers or newspapers without a government, I should not hesitate a moment to prefer the latter."[13] Jefferson saw "the press" as the nation's "only tocsin." If it were "completely silenced ... all means of a general effort [would be] taken away."[14] A "free press" was the vehicle of "public opinion," Jefferson believed, the "force [of which] cannot be resisted when permitted freely to be expressed. The agitation it produces must be submitted to. It is necessary, to keep the waters pure."[15]

Jefferson himself made little or no political use of newspapers, writing in 1796 to George Washington, "From a very early period of my life, I had laid it down as a rule of conduct, never to write a word for the public papers."[16] and cautioning his White House successor, James Madison, that "The Chief Magistrate [ie, the president] cannot enter the arena of the newspapers."[17] It was not until the ascension of Theodore Roosevelt, a century after Jefferson left office, that a president regularly contributed articles to newspapers and magazines, but the real breakthrough in the chief executive's use of mass media to conduct people-to-people government came when Theodore's fifth cousin, Franklin D. Roosevelt, during his tenure as governor of New York, created the "Fireside Chat," an unprecedented use of the still-new medium of radio to broadcast informal addresses directly to the American people. Direct communication with the public became Roosevelt mainstay, and the Fireside Chat would help to carry the nation through multiple crises.

FDR's first fireside chat, as governor, was broadcast on April 3, 1929, just nine years after the very first commercial radio broadcast had been made, in 1920, from Pittsburgh's station KDKA. The growth of radio was rapid, and by the early 1930s, it was the rare American family that did not own or otherwise have regular access to a radio. Calvin Coolidge was first president to broadcast a speech on radio, December 6, 1923. But it was the very formal State of the Union address to a joint session of

Congress. At the end of his first week as president of the United States, on Sunday, March 12, 1933, FDR delivered a very different kind of address, the kind of informal and conversational anti-speech he had honed as new York governor. It was his first national fireside chat, broadcast from the Diplomatic Reception Room of the White House. FDR would go on to make twenty-six more such broadcasts during his presidency. They were talks, addressed conversationally to what was certainly a mass radio audience, but a *mass* audience of *individuals,* whom Roosevelt pictured listening in their parlors. It was a CBS executive, Harry C. Butcher, who coined the highly descriptive phrase "fireside chat" at the time of the second broadcast, on May 7, 1933.

Roosevelt understood that while radio had national, even global reach, it was essentially an intimate medium, one that brought speakers—entertainers, world leaders, it didn't matter which—into the same parlor in which families across America visited with their friends and neighbors. He saw the vehicle of the fireside chat as a powerful way to explain his truly radical economic policies and political programs directly to the people, one on one and one to one. There were no bureaucrats or legislators intervening and no reporter's filtering sensibility getting in the way. There was no need for the pompous and off-putting formality of a conventional political speech. The president's tactic was, usually, to speak on a single issue of pressing importance for fifteen but no more than thirty minutes. Circumstances permitting, he scheduled each chat on a Sunday evening, when most people were at home, together as a family, relaxed, and when audiences were at their biggest—thirty to forty million at a time when the United States population numbered about 130 million. The spontaneous, conversational tone of the fireside chats was actually a carefully crafted effect, as FDR and his staff meticulously prepared each chat through draft after revised draft. What was never contrived, however, was the buoyant optimism that drove most of the chats and the transparent clarity they conveyed.

That first fireside chat, on March 12, 1933, is typical.[18] It focused on an issue of intense and immediate concern to Americans, the banking crisis of the Great Depression. Financial panic had caused a nationwide epidemic of runs on banks as worried depositors rushed to get at their savings before their bank followed others in failure. Officially, FDR coped with the banking crisis by calling a special session of Congress, through which he ushered the Emergency Banking Act, the most important feature of which was a "Bank Holiday," instituted on March 6, which temporarily closed the nation's banks to give them some breathing space, and to enable bank examiners to separate solvent banks from insolvent ones. He used the fireside chat to explain the purpose of the Bank Holiday and to detail the schedule under which sound banks would reopen the following week. It contained no lofty rhetoric, no lecturing, just honesty and clarity, a leader speaking to the people as one citizen to another: "I want to talk for a few minutes with the people of the United States about banking—with the comparatively few who understand the mechanics of banking but more particularly with the overwhelming majority who use banks for the making of deposits and the drawing of checks. I want to tell you what has been done in the last few days, why it was done, and what the next steps are going to be." He acknowledged "that the many proclamations from State Capitols and from Washington, the legislation, the Treasury regulations, etc., couched for the most part in banking and legal terms should be explained for the benefit of the average citizen. I owe this in particular because of the fortitude and good temper with which everybody has accepted the inconvenience and hardships of the banking holiday. I know that when you understand what we in Washington have been about I shall continue to have your cooperation as fully as I have had your sympathy and help during the past week."

FDR used electronic broadcast technology—little more than a decade old at the time—to conduct government people-to-people. At the same time, the national radio networks—CBS, NBC, and Mutual—were just beginning to see themselves as complements to domestic government as well as instruments capable of shaping public diplomacy as well and thereby influencing foreign policy. With the outbreak of World War II in Europe on September 1, 1939, one network, CBS, rapidly came into its own. Whereas NBC based its news on newspapers and Mutual used a small number of newscasters—what the British still call "news readers"—CBS recruited and cultivated a team of professional journalists, who tailored their reports to the new medium. The most memorable of these was Edward R. Murrow, who, during the Blitz—the German air raids on London and other English cities from September 7, 1940, to May 21, 1941—left the network's London studio to venture into the city's streets and even broadcast from rooftops during the height of the bombardment. He vividly related the sights and sensations of the raids while his own microphone also picked up, live, the explosions and the sirens. British wartime regulations compelled civilians in London, including journalists, to take shelter during the air raids. Instantly grasping the power of the broadcast medium to appeal to the people of still-neutral America, Prime Minister Winston Churchill eagerly gave Murrow a permission he withheld even from British reporters, turning him loose on the beleaguered city during raid after raid. As poet and

FDR speechwriter Archibald MacLeish wrote of Murrow in 1941, "You burned the city of London in our houses, and we felt the flames that burned it. You laid the dead of London at our doors, and we knew the dead were our dead."[19]

The person-to-person style of Murrow's reports, coolly but vividly delivered in real time or close to it, had a profound influence on U.S. foreign policy. When Germany invaded Poland on September 1, 1939, triggering the war in Europe, only 20 percent of Americans supported US military aid to Britain and the other Allies opposed to Hitler and Mussolini. By November 1940, a majority favored aiding Britain, even if this meant direct U.S. involvement in the war. A Gallup poll in May 1941 revealed that this majority had expanded to 77 percent of respondents. And in the summer of that year, about 50 percent of Americans rejected any negotation with Germany and a majority believed—despite a relentless record of Nazi victories—that Britain would ultimately emerge victorious. Murrow and other broadcasters were instrumental in this seismic shift of public opinion.[20] Although it was the Japanese attack on Pearl Harbor, Hawaii (at the time a U.S. territory) on December 87, 1941, that prompted a US declaration of war, the vast majority of the American people were by that time enthusiastically receptive to it.

Murrow's live broadcasts during the Blitz were the exception rather than the rule during the 1940s. Although live sportscasting had begun during the infancy of commercial radio, when Detroit's WWJ broadcast the Dempsey-Miske fight on September 6, 1920, most news coverage was studio-based and, typically, recorded ("transcribed" on acetate phonograph recordings) for physical distribution nationally to radio stations and network affiliates for later broadcast. Television, which began commericial network broadcasting in the U.S. in 1948, added to radio the immediacy of video, but the technology was complicated, delicate, and too awkward for most field applications. For years, TV was almost exclusively a studio medium, which relied on film and newsreel techniques for coverage of unfolding current events. As Philip Seib observes in *Real-Time Diplomacy* (Palgrave Macmillan, 2012), the inability of relatively early television news to cover events in real time, especially events overseas, significantly muted the medium's effect on traditional diplomacy. Seib notes that the downside of the "speed of delivery" of real-time reporting is that it is "not always matched by reliability of content." Traditional diplomacy enjoyed what Seib calls a "cushion of time," in which to gather information and deliberately formulate appropriate policy.[21]

Seib looks back to East Germany's closing of the border between East and West Berlin—the beginning of the Berlin Wall—on August 13, 1961. He points out that a CBS TV News crew was present and that the distingusihed reproter Daniel Schorr filmed a report.[22] Had he a smartphone with video and a Twitter connection, events would have flowed out of the border and across the world in real time. But, in 1961, his crew did not even have video tape. The undeveloped newsreel footage of the border closure was driven by car to Berlin's Templehof Airport and put on a regular commercial flight bound for London, where, after a layover of some hours, it was transferred to a trans-Atlantic Pan Am flight to New York. From Idlewild—today John F. Kennedy—International Airport, it was taken to a CBS film-processing lab. By then, sixteen hours had elapsed since the scenes were filmed. Thanks to the time difference between Berlin and New York, it was still Sunday, August 13. But this was raw footage and needed to be edited and produced for national broadcast. By the time this was done, it was Tuesday—and the story finally made the Tuesday *evening* news.

Schorr's report was not only broadcast more than 48 hours after the events, it was also relatively laid back, delivered without the alarming urgency of a live eyewitness account. It surely created public interest in the Berlin events, but it stirred little emotion. The delay in presenting the report meant that, until Tuesday evening, the American public was wholly uninformed, and in this unpressured context, the State Department itself waited some twelve hours to inform President Kennedy, vacationing at the family compound in Hyannis Port, Massachusetts, while analysts tried to assess East German and Soviet intentions associated with the closure. When State Department officials finally contacted the president, he and Secretary of State Dean Rusk had a phone conversation to discuss the US response. Absent either a media or a public demand for immediate action, the two were able to formulate a very measured assessment. The United States had long prepared to respond militarily in the event that the East Germans and/or the Soviets acted to cut off all Berlin—the Western zone of the divided city was a capitalist enclave deep within communist East Germany—from West Germany. That was what happened during the Berlin Blockade of 1948-1949, to which President Truman had responded with the Berlin Airlift. But, this time, all that East German authorities did was to restrict movement between East and West Berlin. The Allied corridors through East Germany to West Berlin remained wide open. Instead of focusing on what East Germany had done, Kennedy and his secretary of state took into account what it had *not* done. They therefore decided that the East German action posed no immediate threat and required no immediate action.

None of this meant that the US government stood down. Rather, as Seib puts it, "The president's low-key reaction ... bought time for more information to be gathered."[23] As more insight was developed, the president and his advisors concluded that the beginning of construction of what became the Berlin Wall did not represent a major shift in Soviet policy and therefore did not warrant a provocative Allied military response. The wisdom of this decision might be debated today. But could the United States have done anything to stop the construction of the Wall without risking a bloody response in Berlin and, subsequently, a wider conflict between the two nuclear superpowers? True, walled Berlin would remain a tripwire and a hot spot for nearly the next three decades. True, families were divided within the city and suffered as a result. True, too, at least 136 persons were killed in attempts to defeat the Berlin Wall and escape to West (at least one estimate puts the death toll closer to 1,200).[24] But no wider conflict was triggered, and, for some twenty-eight years, the Berlin Wall stood as a shameful confession of Communist tyranny and failure. In terms of global propaganda, it was a self-inflicted wound. Indeed, the Berlin Wall finally "fell" in November 1989, it was universally interpreted as the herald of the Soviet empire's fall. Had the events of August 1961 taken place in the context of the communications technology of the second decade of the twenty-first century, Seib and others speculate, both broadcast and cable TV networks would be providing live coverage, with cable doing so on a 24-hour cycle. YouTube would feature smartphone videos made by spectators on both sides of the Wall, and Twitter would issue a torrent of 140-character real-time messages. These Internet sources, generated by "citizen journalists," would be selectively picked up by commercial media and packaged as urgent "Breaking News" bulletins, accompanied by dramatically scripted commentary and even portentous theme music. Since all of this would be happening in real time or close to it, there would be no "cushion of time" in which to analyze, assess, and communicate "context related to larger geopolitical issues."[25]

Public diplomacy and the emergence of real-time technology

By the time US involvement in the Vietnam War was in full swing, television news coverage had improved technologically over what was available in 1961. Although coverage was still mainly dependent on film rather than video tape and rarely featured live reporting from the field, the flow of television news coverage was voluminous and daily, so that Vietnam has often been described as history's "first televised war."[26]

Certainly, the administration of Lyndon Johnson was aware of the power of the media, especially television, and was determined to use it to counter the antiwar movement that became increasingly strident, populous, and influential in the long course of the war. Beginning early in 1967, the administration launched what was widely called a "media offensive," which was fronted by General William Westmoreland. The top US commander in Vietnam, Westmoreland was called home from his Saigon headquarters to present US military achievements and progress in the war. Through televised press conferences and interviews, he argued that US and South Vietnamese (ARVN) forces were inflicting losses that clearly outpaced enemy recruitment and reinforcement. By the numbers, the attrition was undeniable, he claimed. Westmoreland and other administration officials also defended the much-maligned "pacification program," an often brutal campaign directed against South Vietnamese civilians and aimed at rooting out popular support for the Viet Cong in the South.

Whereas the most effective network TV news coverage often relied on isolated images of war, Westmoreland offered overall "facts and figures." Regarding pacification, for instance, he presented estimates that 800,000 to 1,000,000 South Vietnamese villagers had been "liberated" from Communist control in 1966 alone. He noted that, in 1965, Communist insurgents had closed 70 percent of South Vietnam's roadways and waterways, but that, by the beginning of 1967, 60 percent were open.

Surprisingly, few challenged the credibility and accuracy of Westmoreland's data. Yet, in the end, the data hardly mattered. The disparity between the statistics and the clearly apparent lack of movement toward peace suggested to a growing number of Americans that the war was at a permanent stalemate. President Johnson continued to assure television viewers that there was "light at the end of the tunnel," but the mounting number of U.S. casualties—the only numbers that really mattered to most of the public—created what the press dubbed a "credibility gap" between what the administration claimed and what the American people believed.

Increasingly, Americans became divided between those who opposed the war and those who continued to support it. In Congress, this translated into a division between "doves" (opponents of the war) and "hawks" (the war's supporters). With each passing month, the ranks of the doves rose, as did the volume of their voices. When Congress formally proposed to the administration a vigorous peace initiative in the autumn of 1967, Secretary of State Dean Rusk called a news conference on October 12, claiming that such initiatives were futile because North Vietnam would not entertain them. This response did nothing to quell antiwar sentiment, and all Johnson and Westmoreland could do was to continue to assert that progress was being made. On November 21, Westmoreland declared to reporters: "I am absolutely certain that whereas in 1965 the enemy was winning, today he is certainly losing."

Viewed strictly in military terms, there was truth to this claim. Military progress was being made. Militarily, the North was undeniably suffering substantially more casualties than the combined US and ARVN forces. Yet neither the American president nor the American commander in charge seemed willing to acknowledge that, as far as an increasing segment of the American public was concerned, these military truths were entirely beside the point. What *was* the point? The North Vietnamese continually manifested a limitless capacity for absorbing losses. They were clearly willing to die for their cause, and to die in numbers much greater than those who opposed them.

Still, Johnson continued to wage his "media offensive" by making heavy use of television, the very medium that was providing the American public with extensive news coverage of the war. Whereas the Korean War (1950-1953) had taken place during television's infancy and was therefore reported mainly by newspapers, Vietnam exploded during the first great heyday of televised news. By the middle of 1965, all of the major networks opened Saigon bureaus, which grew into the third largest they maintained, behind only New York and Washington. No wonder that historians of television and popular culture often remark that television coverage of Vietnam helped to create the antiwar movement by bringing into the nation's living rooms graphic images of the horrors of war.

And there were plenty of horrors to present.

In August 1965, CBS aired a report showing US Marines casually igniting the thatched roofs of the village of Cam Ne with Zippo lighters. Yet what is often forgotten in recent accounts of the "first televised war" is that most TV reporting actually *avoided* presenting scenes of atrocity or bloodshed—at least until the very end of the 1960s. Up to the period of the 1968 Tet Offensive, in fact, war coverage was mostly upbeat and typically relayed to viewers whatever military spokespeople provided to reporters in daily press briefings. Indeed, most of the coverage was rather abstract, given the concrete nature of the medium. Reports were read by the news anchors and typically illustrated not with combat footage, but by battle maps. Although casualty figures were reported, generally on a weekly basis, the US casualty count was always accompanied by the enemy "body count," which greatly exceeded the losses incurred by American forces. From its earliest days, American television covered a wide array of sporting events, and viewers were accustomed to keeping score. Numbers-oriented coverage of the Vietnam War throughout most of the 1960s consistently made it appear that America was winning.

On January 30, 1968, North Vietnamese forces launched a broad and massive offensive coinciding with Tet, a Vietnamese lunar holiday.[27] US and ARVN forces were caught flat footed by the attacks, but nevertheless responded to them very effectively. Although the ancient Vietnamese capital, Hue, fell to communist forces, all of the other initial gains made by the North Vietnamese Army (NVA) and the Viet Cong (VC) were reversed within days of the initial onslaught. As for body count, approximately 15,515 Communist fighters were killed during January 28–February 3, whereas 416 U.S. and 784 ARVN troops (as well as 3,071 South Vietnamese civilians) died. Thus nearly 15 NVA/VC troops died for every U.S./ARVN soldier killed in the opening phase of the offensive. Far worse for the Communists, the offensive failed to trigger the general southern uprising its planners had counted on.

By any tactical standard, US and ARVN forces triumphed in Tet. Both President Johnson and General Westmoreland attempted to portray Tet as a failed act of communist desperation, clear evidence that the North was fatally weakened. Yet Washington proved unable to "spin" Tet as a *strategic* victory. The year just ended, 1967, had seen the balance of public opinion turn against the war. Now, to a growing majority of Americans, Tet said two things: First, despite what Johnson and Westmoreland claimed, the massive Tet attacks hardly appeared to be the work of a moribund enemy. As America's most popular and trusted television news anchor, Walter Cronkite, asked, "What the hell is going on? I thought we were winning the war?" Second, the scope and intensity of the Tet attacks seemed like dramatic evidence of North Vietnamese unity and commitment. For many Americans, the NVA and VC were beginning to look like nationalist heroes and freedom fighters, not just a highly determined enemy.

In the days, weeks, and months following the initial Tet onslaught, American TV news began to focus on evidence of ARVN (and even US) combat brutality. The single most stunning image was the photograph by Eddie Adams of the Associated Press (AP), taken on February 1, 1968, showing the chief of South Vietnam's national police, Colonel Nguyen Ngoc Loan, summarily executing a Viet Cong prisoner with a single .38-caliber shot to the head. Everything about the image was obscene: the setting in the middle of an otherwise peaceful Saigon intersection; the businesslike demeanor of the chief; the plaid short-sleeve shirt of the suspect (no uniform), his hands tied behind him; the grotesque contortion of the man's face as the bullet entered his skull. This single image, accurately or not, revealed a hardened enemy to be no more than a slightly built youngster and, to all appearances, an innocent, helpless victim.

Moreover, while Tet was an overwhelming US-ARVN tactical victory, the American public saw images of horror and atrocity and a US casualty rate that had risen from 780 per month during 1967 to 2,000 in February 1968. When a somewhat-distorted news story broke in March, announcing that General Westmoreland wanted an additional 200,000 men committed to the war, a wave of outrage swept the American public. Antiwar demonstrations became bigger, angrier, and more numerous. By the middle of March, public opinion polls revealed that 70 percent of Americans favored a phased withdrawal of US forces from Vietnam, and, at the end of the month, President Johnson initiated a process designed to withdraw the United States from the war. Although Westmoreland never received the number of troops he wanted, American forces peaked at 536,000 by the end of 1968.

As troop withdrawals began in 1969, television coverage increasingly reflected the growing skepticism among journalists concerning government claims of progress and the "light at the end of the tunnel." Moreover, whereas pre-Tet coverage of the antiwar movement had been slim and mostly critical, after Tet, the movement was being portrayed as a legitimate, even mainstream, political movement. Opposition to the war was portrayed as the norm, whereas support for it was made to appear extreme and even aberrant.

Television coverage of the Vietnam War reflected changing public opinion at least as much as it shaped it. In this, it was both an echo chamber and a source of information. To lawmakers and policymakers, the television medium delivered coverage both of the war in Vietnam and the war at home—the growing discontent of the American electorate. Beyond question, television thus affected both public opinion and the decision making process taking place in Washington. It was thus truly a medium of people-to-people government and, insofar as this influenced foreign policy, it was also public diplomacy. But the effect of the television medium was gradual. It had shaped public sentiment and political decisions over a period of months and even years. It influenced an evolution rather than a revolution in direction.

Typically, the televised Vietnam War reached the American people only for a half-hour each day, during the evening news. At the time, this seemed like a heavy enough dose of misery. On June 1, 1980, five years after the Vietnam War had ended, a maverick media mogul from Atlanta named Ted Turner would up the news dosage to 24 hours and seven days a week. Having inherited—and revived—his father's outdoor advertising business, Ted Turner acquired two failing UHF television stations, one in 1970 and another in 1972, and turned them into successes, partly by persuading advertisers that viewers of UHF were more intelligent and commanded higher incomes than viewers of standard VHF. In 1975, he took notice when cable TV pioneer HBO announced that it would soon begin transmitting its signal to a new communications satellite, which would bounce the signal back to receiving dishes owned by American cable distributors, who would, in turn, distribute the programming to cable subscribers all over the United States. In this way, HBO would be as *national* a television presence as any of the big established broadcast networks. Inspired, Turner decided to make one of his UHF stations, WTCG, Channel 17, the first local *broadcast* station to go national by sending its signal to a satellite and bouncing it to America's cable distributors. He launched the enterprise the following year as the SuperStation. Its programming consisted mostly of a library of old ("classic") films he was in the process of amassing, plus coverage of baseball—he owned the Atlanta Braves. Within two years, he bought the Atlanta Hawks basketball team as well, and also began broadcasting their games.

Just one thing, Turner decided, was missing: news. And it was not missing just from the SuperStation. As Turner saw it, news—*national news*—was all but missing on broadcast television itself. It occupied just one-half hour (22 minutes plus commercials) each evening. Ted Turner proposed to use a satellite/cable station to give the nation what no one else was giving it: 24 hours of news, seven days a week. Turner began to gather a small cadre of non-network, but television-savvy news experts. Working with them, he put together the formula and the logistics of a 24-hour news station. When he initially presented the idea to cable operators, few were willing to pony up the modest subscription fee he asked for. But Turner persisted and, on May 21, 1979, announced to the convention of the National Cable Television Association that CNN, the Cable News Network, would be launched on June 1, 1980. He explained that his intention was to realize the promise of television that media guru Marshall McLuhan had written about in the 1960s: the transformation of the whole world into a "global village." This vision won over the cable providers, and CNN was launched. A decade later, when President George H. W. Bush took the United States and a coalition of allies into war against Saddam Hussein's Iraq, which had invaded Kuwait and threatened Saudi Arabia, CNN was extraordinarily well positioned to cover the conflict.

If Vietnam was the first televised war, the Gulf War of 1990-1991 was the first war to be televised on a 24/7 cycle. Not only did CNN coverage influence US public perception of the war, but, providing news to more than a hundred countries, CNN was a potent influencer of global public opinion. Indeed, governments and militaries—including those of the United States and its allies—closely monitored CNN for open source intelligence to supplement their own closed intelligence and diplomatic channels. At times, diplomats deliberately used CNN to deliver messages that could not be conveyed via official channels. After throwing other news organizations out of Baghdad, Saddam Hussein allowed CNN reporters to remain—presumably because he saw CNN as a necessary communications pipeline to Bush. Ted Turner remarked, "If there's a chance for peace … it might come through us. Hell, both siders aren't talking to each other, but they're talking to CNN. We have a major responsibility."[28]

In general, coverage of the Gulf War was seen as a history-making triumph for CNN, and it prompted other broadcast organizations to get into the 24-hour news business. Yet some commentators were critical. Lawrence Grossman, the former president of NBC News, a traditional television news operation, condemned at least some of the 24/7 coverage as "the illusion of news," remarking that the raw on-the-scene images and sound bites "at times served to mask reality" by delivering "Rumors, gossip, speculation, hearsay and unchecked claims" without the time-consuming due diligence of verification and sourcing. Grossman complained that CNN "reporters wondered aloud on-screen about what they were seeing and what was happening" instead of acting like professional journalists, whose responsibility it was to "filter out true information from false."[29] In truth, CNN reporters were often witnesses rather than journalists. In this, however, they brought a global cable news audience to bear witness alongside them. To be sure, this arrangement tended to create dramatic impressions rather than measured insight. Was the public sentiment it stimulated productive, destructive, ambiguous, or meaningless? Moreover, whereas government officials, including traditional diplomats, were accustomed to weighing journalistic reports in formulating decisions and taking actions, the relentless and relentlessly unfiltered 24/7 immediacy of CNN meant (as Scheib observes) that "policymakers [now had to] deal with journalism that violates the old rule, 'Get it first, but first get it right.'"[30]

The doubts and dangers notwithstanding, CNN coverage of the Gulf War ensured that unfiltered, real-time television coverage of world events was a genie released and never to be rebottled. As Scheib put it, gone forever was the era "in which diplomats talked only to diplomats" and did so essentially at their leisure. "This is a new time, and new diplomatic practices must be developed that can succeed in the real-time era."[31]

Mr. Bezos, tear down this wall

What even the most prescient diplomats of 1991 could not predict—not even those who accepted the necessity of dealing with "news" broadcast unfiltered and in real time from the very heart of roiling chaos—was the coming impact of technolgies that would create vast legions of "citizen journalists." By the beginning of the twenty-first century, a dozen or twenty or a hundred CNN field correspondents would be multiplied into thousands or tens of thousands of ordinary people distinguished only by their possession of a smartphone video camera and a Twitter account or access to YouTube.

As CNN earned far more plaudits than criticism, so would these "citizen journalists" (as we will see in the next chapter). But much as such traditional television journalists as Lawrence Grossman voiced doubts about CNN, so traditional diplomats worried about how aggregated, amplified, and ramified realtime reporting would influence public opinion, which, in turn, would force upon policymakers suboptimal or even disastrous decisions. Most notable among these critical voices was that of George Kennan, dean of the postwar US diplomatic corps, the leading theorist and architect of US Cold War policy. After watching the televised landing of US troops in Somalia, Kennan attrributed public support for military intervention to television "exposure of the Somalia situation." He worried that "American policy from here on out, particularly policy involving the uses of our armed forces abroad" would be "controlled by popular emotional impulses ... especially ones provoked by the commericial television industry." Should this occur, he wrote, "then there is no place not only for myself, but for the responsible deliberative organs of our government ..."[32]

Kennan assumed that CNN and the imitators it had spawned would excite "emotional impulses" in the public, who, in turn, would accordingly and irresistibly press for particular policies and actions. Like other worried diplomats, he had no way of knowing that, in the new century, the mediation even of unfiltered 24/7 television would no longer be necessary to provoke impulses and create the public will. Just two years before Kennan's book appeared, in 1994, Jeff Bezos left the Wall Street investment management firm of which he was vice president, moved from New York to Seattle, and laid out the company that would go online in 1995 as Amazon.com. Heeding predictions of an impending meteoric rise in Internet commerce, Bezos wanted to claim a first-mover advantage and launched Amazon as a gargantuan online bookstore. The company not only weathered the dot-com bubble of the late 1990s and early 2000s, it grew exponentially, expanding from books to virtually every kind of merchandise traditionally sold by mail-order or brick-and-mortar merchants.

Eventually, Amazon began to outsell, displace, or coopt many of these traditional merchants. The advantages Amazon offered consumers included virtually limitless variety, total transparency as to pricing and price comparison among products as well as vendors, the instant availability of consumer as well as expert product reviews, effortless billing, effortless shipping, easy returns, and the overall convenience of a virtually frictionless online experience. For consumers as well as vendors, manufacturers, and merchants, it was liberating. President Ronald Reagan had dramatized the imminence of political liberation when, speaking to an audience gathered at the Berlin Wall on June 12, 1987, he suddenly addressed the leader of the Soviet Union: "Mr. Gorbachev, tear down this wall!" A few years later, Jeff Bezos's Amazon was introducing the world to global commerce with the walls suddenly torn down.

This commericial liberation was made possible by the personal computer and the Internet. But, extraordinary as this was, there was more "liberation technology" to come. In 2011, smartphone sales worldwide overtook sales of PCs.[33] By the start of 2014, Americans were using their smartphones and tablets more than their PCs to access the Internet.[34] Two years earlier, the authors of *Trillions: Thriving in the Emerging Information Ecology,* had gone so far as to proclaim, "as a consumer product, the PC is dead—as dead as the eight-track tape cartridge"[35]

As the personal computer liberated humanity from the room-sized mainframe and as the laptop liberated us from the desktop, so the smartphone sets everyone free to have a computer, a recording device (still and video), and an Internet connection literally in hand anywhere that hand and its attached body may find themselves. As Amazon liberated us from the shopping mall, the smartphone liberates us from the necessity of having go wherever our computers are to make an online purchase. Transactions can now be done via smartphone—anywhere. Given the right app, we are even free, in our increasingly rare wanderings through the brick-and-mortar world, to use our smartphone camera to scan a bar code on any merchandise we encounter—or even snap a picture of the product itself—and buy it online. More and more brick-and-mortar merchants have stopped fighting liberation technology and have instead enlisted it. Thanks to near-field communications technology, our smartphones are free to tell us when we are passing a store or a store shelf that offers merchandise in which, somewhere at some time, we expressed an interest.

But the liberation of mobile liberation technology goes far beyond the world of wall-less commerce.

The revolution will be tweeted

Let me confess that I have hijacked—up to this point, at any rate—the very phrase "liberation technology." Its intended use is not as a label for digital commerce, but to describe what Hoover Institution senior fellow Larry Diamond calls "a striking ability of the Internet … to empower individuals, facilitate independent communication and mobilization, and strengthen an emergent civil society." Diamond explains: "Liberation technology enables citizens to report news, expose wrongdoing, express opinions, mobilize protest, monitor elections, scrutinize government, deepen participation, and expand the horizons of freedom. . . . Liberation technology is any form of information communication technology (ICT) that can expand political, social, and economic freedom."[36]

Diamond narrates a "watershed" instance of the Internet as "liberation technology," a notable occasion on which it was used to channel "a peaceful outpouring of public opinion [to compel] the Communist Chinese state to change a national regulation."[37] In March 2003, police in Guangzhou (Canton) arrested twenty-seven-year-old Sun Zhigang, demanding to see his temporary living permit and identification. Unable to produce these documents, he was packed off to a detention facility, where, three days later, he died in an infirmary. The cause of death, officials recorded, was a heart attack. Sun's parents, however, ordered an autopsy, which revealed evidence of a severe beating. This sent the young man's father and mother to a lcoal liberal newspaper, *Southern Metropolis Daily,* which launched an investigation that confirmed the beating. The local story was quickly picked up by newspapers and websites throughout China, and it became a national story as "chat rooms and bulletin boards exploded with outrage."[38]

"The central government was forced to launch its own investigation and on June 27 [2003], it found twelve people guilty of Sun's death."[39] Remarkably, this instance of the application of liberation technology also "had a much wider and more lasting impact, provoking national debate about the 'Custody and Repatriation' (C&R) measures that allowed the police to detain rural immigrants (typically in appalling consitions) for lacking a residency or temporary-living permit." The Internet stories about Sun's death prompted "numerous Chinese citizens" to post Internet accounts of their own traumatic run-ins with C&R. Universities began debating the constitutionality of C&R legislation, a petition to the Standing Committee of the National People's Congress was drawn up, and in June 2003 the government announced that it would close all— more than 800—C&R detention centers.[40]

The Internet amplified and ramified the Sun case until it produced a signficant legal and policy change. It was the kind of change that points the way toward digitally enabled public diplomacy—call it cyberdiplomacy—although it was still well short of revolutionary. However, the events of the so-called Arab Spring (in the Mideast region itself, "Arab Awakening" is the preferred term) have been widely interpreted as the genuinely revolutionary application of liberation technology on a scale that is regional and therefore transnational. Insofar as it crossed borders, ecompassed a vast region, and rippled throughout the world, the application of digital technology in the Arab Awakening also transcended conventional government as well as conventional diplomacy.

With an implied nod to the 1970 Gil Scott-Heron song, "The Revolution Will Not Be Televised, former Peace Corps volunteer and independent scholar Mario Machado wrote a 2013 *Huffington Post* piece titled "The Revolution Will Be Tweeted." He began, "The next revolution will certainly be televised, but, when it is, it will already be old news. Long before the cameras and the reporters arrive in the midst of the action, it will hjave been Facebook-ed and tweeted and Instagram-ed around the entire planet, probablty even before any one has any idea what's really going on."[41]

This fact alone—the realtime aggregation of raw eyewitness documentation and its realtime dissemnation, raw, across the global Internet—will demand that governments and diplomats take note, respond, and even race in a desperate and probably doomed effort to draw abreast of events, let alone get ahead of them. Add to this the full potential of the *liberation* part of "liberation technology," especially the use of mobile devices on the Internet not merely to tweet the revolution but to organize and lead it, and the necessity of cyberdiplomacy becomes urgently apparent.

The next chapter explores both the potential and the actual performance of the Internet, digital devices, and the people using them to create, in some cases, liberation and in others, terror. The chapter that follows it explores the limitations of that technology.

CHAPTER 2
PEOPLE POWER 2.0

Born into the Filipino oligarchy, Benigno Aquino Jr. nevertheless became a champion of struggling democracy in the Philippines. At the age of twenty-two, he was elected mayor of Concepcion, in the province of Tarlac, later became vice governor and then governor of the province, and from 1967 to 1972, a senator. Throughout his career in the Senate, he was a relentless critic of the corrupt dictatorship of President Ferdinand Marcos. Aquino was imprisoned by Marcos—bizarrely charged with murder, subversion, and illegal possession of firearms—protested with a Gandhi-like hunger strike, and endured incarceration, mostly in solitary confinement, as his trial dragged out. During all of this, he remained the powerful symbolic leader of his country's democracy movement. Sentenced to death by firing squad in November 1977, Aquino remained in his cell while the verdict was appealed. But in March 1980, he suffered a heart attack and was transported to the Philippine Heart Center, but refused to submit to bypass surgery for fear that Marcos would use his surgeons as the instruments of his murder. He informed the regime that he preferred either treatment in the United States or return to his cell to face death, either as a result of his ailing heart or the bullets of a firing squad.

In the mistaken belief that American exile would effectively neutralize Aquino, Marcos allowed him to go. After a successful surgery, he toured the United States, building in this country popular and political support for his struggle against the Marcos regime. In 1983, sensing that Marcos was politically vulnerable, and after seven years and seven months of imprisonment and three years of exile, Aquino decided to return to his homeland. He knew that he was facing probable assassination, telling one of the journalists who accompanied him on his August 21 flight that he should be "very ready with [his] hand camera because this action can become very fast. In a matter of a three or four minutes it could be all over, you know, and"—he laughed—"I may not be able to talk to you again after this."[42]

Awaiting Aquino's arrival in Manila was what Marcos called a "bodyguard" of a thousand soldiers and police officers. When the aircraft pulled up to a Manila International arrival gate at 1:04 in the afternoon, government troops boarded, arrested Aquino, and led him toward a military vehicle for transport to prison. Before the party reached the vehicle, shots rang out, and Aquino lay dead on the tarmac apron.

Without doubt, Aquino had been shot on orders of Marcos. But the dictator quickly lost control of the aftermath of the assassination. Aquino's body lay in state in a glass coffin, a gaping bullet wound on his face. The funeral parlor was open to the public, who came in long lines to pay their respects. The funeral itself, on August 31, drew more than two million into the streets of the capital. It was the beginning of a popular uprising dubbed the "People Power Revolution," and it carried Ninoy Aquino's widow, Corazon "Cory" Aquino, to victory over Marcos three years later, in the presidential elections of 1986.

People Power II and 2.0

Corazon Aquino served until 1992 and was succeeded by Fidel Ramos, who continued her reforms. In 1998, Ramos was succeeded by Joseph Estrada, who earned the dubious distinction of tenth place on Transparency International's 2004 *Global Corruption Report* listing the "All-Time Most Corrupt Leaders in the World" (Marcos earned second place, behind 1967-1998 Indonesian president Suharto).[43]

In January 2001, digital technology, including the Internet and mobile phones, organized millions of Filipinos into a protest against Estrada's corruption. Howard Rheingold, author of *Smart Mobs: The Next Social Revolution,* called this a "smart mob" and pronounced Estrada "the first head of state in history to lose power" to one.[44] Within weeks, impeachment proceedings commenced. Even these were "fueled in part by anti-Estrada information found on more than 200 websites and about 100 e-mail discussion groups."[45]

In its impeachment investigation, the Philippine Senate refused to consider some of the evidence found online and elsewhere. The refusal catalyzed the anti-Estrada movement as "People Power II," a revival of and successor to the 1986 anti-Marcos movement that had made Corazon Aquino president. In the Internet age, however, People Power II might well have been dubbed People Power 2.0. For mobile phones coordinated mass action, one SMS operator reporting 45 million messages daily, about double the usual load, and another handling 70 million messages in the week during which the protest was organized.[46]

Political sociologist and Hoover Institution fellow Larry Diamond called the networked technological apparatus of People Power II "Liberation Technology."[47] The SMS messaging during the movement ran the gamut from organizational logistics (telling people where and when to gather, for example), to informational website links, to "jokes about Estrada's personal life,"[48] and there is no doubt that this application of "liberation technology" contributed to the removal of Estrada from office. The original People Power movement in 1986 was propelled by the assassination of the popular Ninoy Aquino and the appeal of his unassuming but charismatic widow, Corazon. Nevertheless, the movement had to contend with a mass media in the Philippines that was tightly controlled by Marcos. People Power II had neither a martyr nor a particularly charismatic rival to Estrada, but it did have widespread outrage against rampant corruption, and it had the decentralized force of Internet and mobile communication. Nevertheless, the overthrow of Estrada was not simply the product of a technologically enabled popular uprising. Estrada's corruption was such that he lost not only popular support but that of most of the rest of the government and other Philippine institutions. In short, the entire Estrada administration was weak and vulnerable. "Liberation technology" provided the final push that sent it toppling.

Certainly, the push came quickly, propelled by the speed and reach of the Internet and the millions of mobile nodes connected to it. From People Power II in 2001 through the first decade of the twenty-first century and into the second, Internet technology, especially mobile technology become increasingly sophisticated with the development of the smartphone, has played an important role in creating antigovernment networks in Ecuador, Ukraine, and South Korea, and in the uprisings of what Westerners dubbed the Arab Spring (and most activists in the Middle East call the Arab Awakening). This includes antigovernment movements in Tunisia, Egypt, Libya, Yemen, and Syria.

"Twitter revolutions"

Many—especially Westerners on the outside looking in—have been quick to identify a central role for social media and mobile platforms in fomenting and driving the uprisings of the Arab Spring. Some have applied the phrase "Twitter Revolutions" to the uprisings in Tunisia (2010-2011) and Egypt (in 2011), as well as to popular unrest and revolt in Iran (the election protests of 2009-2010) and, outside of the Middle

East, to the election protests in Moldava (2009) and the so-called Euromaidan Revolution in Ukraine (2013-2014). In an acerbic *New Yorker* essay published on February 2, 2011, Malcolm Gladwell expressed his reservations about the West's wide-eyed eagerness to ascribe all recent popular opposition to the status quo to the "miracle" of Twitter, Facebook, and smartphones.[49] As we will see in the next chapter, Gladwell's skeptical voice concerning the political omnipotence of the Internet is just one of many. This said, it cannot be denied that social media and mobile technology figured prominently in the Arab Spring.

Tunisia is a prime example, and in a discussion of *Distant Witness: Social Media, the Arab Spring, and a Journalism Revolution*, at the time a forthcoming book by National Public Radio's senior product manager for online communities, Andy Carvin, Colin Delany reported on a discussion at NPR's Washington, DC headquarters led by a young Tunisian protester named Rim Nour. As Delany commented, the discussion "provided fantastic details on how Tunisians used technology to accelerate their revolution, and in the process gave us a preview of how other people around the world might do the same."[50]

A Tunisian with a background in technology and public policy who bore witness to the "Jasmine Revolution" of 2010-2011, Nour argued that social media did not foment the revolution, but certainly accelerated it. Perhaps even more importantly, digital tools helped Tunisians organize in ways that protected the political gains that had been made.

Tunisia was and remains a country with a young, well-educated population struggling in an environment that offered few jobs in general and far fewer for graduates with secondary and college degrees. Many of its citizens were enthusiastic users of Internet technology, with 85 percent of the population using cell phones—and 5 percent smartphones. About 2 million of Tunisia's 10 million residents and 2 million expats were on Facebook. Judged strictly by the numbers, Twitter in 2010 had such a user base so mall—500 active within the country—as to disqualify that "Twitter Revolution" sobriquet. But Nour argued that the raw number is misleading because most of the very few Tunisians who tweeted were seasoned political activists, who knew how to leverage Twitter to produce a social impact far beyond the platform's minimal presence within the country's borders. A more difficult impediment was the government's censorship of YouTube and other major channels.

Nour explained to those who attended the NPR conference that Tunisia's "Jasmine Revolution" developed in three main phases. The first consisted of protests in the Tunisian interior, sparked by the public self-immolation of Mohamed Bouazizi. A street merchant in the rural town of Sidi Bouzid, Bouazizi eked out a living with his vegetable cart until December 17, 2010, when a policewoman seized the cart (for want of the required license), together with his merchandise. Bouazizi went to the local administrative authorities seeking the return of the cart and contents, but the officials refused even to see him. Rebuffed, Bouazizi left the administrative building and returned a short time later. Dousing himself with an unidentified flammable liquid, he set himself ablaze outside of the building. He lingered, gravely burned, in the local hospital, unaware that he had become the inspiration for mass demonstrations against the regime of President Zine el Abidine Ben Ali throughout the country.

The protests provoked a brutal police response, which Tunisians captured with their cell phone video cameras. Using Twitter and other means, activists saw to it that these images were broadcast online, both within Tunisia and, soon, throughout the region and the world. The dissemination of the response to Bouazizi-inspired protests and the government's attempts to suppress them initiated the second phase of the revolution. Tunisians all across the country—including its most affluent and well-educated areas—poured into the streets of Sfax and Tunis. A new "smart mob" took shape as the protesters used their cell phones and Facebook to organize themselves. The uprising soon became sufficiently intense to prompt President Ben Ali to flee the country. At this point, Tunisia teetered on the verge of violent anarchy, but (Nour said) the people used social media to scotch rumors and to further organize themselves to fight government security forces and diehard Ben Ali supporters as well as a fringe of violent protestors and looters.

It is important to note that the dramatic self-immolation of Bouazizi provided the human, emotional spark of revolution—the tragic visual material that quickly went viral, organized by Tunisia's tiny cadre of Twitter users under a #Bouazizi hashtag. The spread of the movement from the impoverished interior to the more prosperous urban areas took no more than two weeks. At this point, Nour reported, Facebook became the center of action online. Whereas Twitter had but 500 users in Tunisia, Facebook had some two million, and they made extensive use of the videos that flowed in from the streets.

Facebook exposure also ensured that the Tunisian events would be seen across the world, not only among Westerners but also by a Tunisian expat community of at least two million. Operating far beyond the reach of any government censorship, these activists brought the Jasmine Revolution to the attention of the global mass media (especially Al Jazeera TV), news organizations, and governments. The global response, in turn, echoed strongly back in Tunisia, bolstering and building the movement there.

The Tunisian government embarked on a desperate media counteroffensive, not via the Internet but using the television and radio networks in controlled. By this time, however, the conventionally broadcast stories became easy targets for social media activists, who readily poked holes in the lies and propaganda. As Nour pointed out, when government-controlled television broadcast images of a pro-Ben Ali demonstration, Jasmine revolutionaries were able to post on Facebook their own video footage, revealing just how few Ben Ali supporters actually demonstrated.

Nour explained that social channels became vital in shaping revolutionary activity even in a highly fluid situation. When protestors were taken into custody, for example, social media coverage prompted other activists to argue promptly for their release. In addition, well-informed activists used social media to correct and counteract rumors, misinformation, and outright disinformation. The same online digital technology that amplified Bouazizi's desperate act of protest into a revolution kept the revolution alive, focused, and mostly non-violent. Still, Nour insisted, social media did not *create* the Tunisian revolution. It *enabled* it.

Interactive social media, with mobile technology, did not replace traditional broadcast mass media during the Arab Spring. In some cases, where the mass media was government controlled, social media provided a more trusted and trustworthy means of communications. Outside of Tunisia, in places where mass media was freer and more trusted, social media provided a source of information. Video from individual citizen cell phones was posted on websites and then picked up by major broadcasters worldwide. Thus, in many instances, social media and broadcast media developed a synergistic relationship.

Digitally enhanced networks

Underlying it all—the Internet and mobile technology as well as its amplification through conventional broadcast media—is the concept of networks. These webs of interpersonal relationships are greatly enhanced by social media platforms and the infrastructure of the Internet; however, they are made up of offline, face-to-face, official and informal relationships as well as virtual connections online. The networks that drive political change consist of personal relationships as well as relationships between and among institutions, governments, and departments within governments. While both offline and online networks often cross state borders and administrative or bureaucratic boundaries, the technology of online networking makes such transcendence easier, deeper, and wider. The proliferation of the Internet did not create networking, but it has certainly intensified and multiplied it. Skilled diplomats have long recognized the importance of unofficial relationships and "back channels." During the Cuban Missile Crisis of 1962, for example, it was a trusted back channel, via ABC newsman John Scali, that connected the White House with a trusted Soviet back-channel contact and ultimately allowed the leadership of the United States and the USSR to talk and thereby avert thermonuclear war. The phenomenal proliferation of networks enabled by the Internet requires diplomats and policymakers to be even more willing and savvy in reaching out to exploit informal contacts and back channels.

In the case of the Arab Spring, the Internet facilitated the exchange of information among activists and made it possible to respond to real-world social and political developments in something very close to real time. In addition, mobile technology and the Internet—especially the interface between the Internet and conventional broadcast media—brought the whole world into events taking place in the Middle East. This, in turn, engaged expat communities worldwide and influenced public opinion as well as government policy in the West and elsewhere.

Writing in 2011, Internet socio-economist Clay Shirky observed that the more developed Internet-enabled networks become, the more information they open to "the networked population," providing "more opportunities to engage in public speech … and … undertake collective action." Shirky believes that Internet-enabled networking "can help loosely coordinated publics demand change."[51]

Implicit in Shirky's analysis is a view of Internet networking as inherently open and decentralized. As Charlie Beckett wrote in 2011, the Internet networks in Tunisia and Egypt during the Arab Spring were organized around "nodal figures who all tended to resist conventional leadership roles." Beckett in part ascribed what he called the "diffuse, horizontal nature" of the Arab Spring movements to the decentralized nature of the Internet itself, and he judged this structure "very difficult [for governments] to break."[52]

"Dispersed but still connected," Philip Seib writes in *Real-Time Diplomacy,* "that is the basic geography of networks. It was a perfect model for the agents of change during the Arab Spring."[53] This point of view harks back to the early visions of the Internet as a kind of anti-government government or, more precisely, the replacement of government with what the pre-digital (1911-1972) social critic/anarchist philosopher Paul Goodman called in the title of a 1947 book, "communitas."[54] On February 8, 1996, which Electronic Frontier Foundation founding member (and sometime Grateful Dead lyricist)

John Perry Barlow published "A Declaration of the Independence of Cyberspace," which began: "Governments of the Industrial World, you weary giants of flesh and steel, I come from Cyberspace, the new home of Mind. On behalf of the future, I ask you of the past to leave us alone. You are not welcome among us. You have no sovereignty where we gather."[55]

At the time, Barlow's declaration may have seemed extreme, yet also powerful and even inevitable—a statement of present fiat but imminent fact: "I declare the global social space we are building to be naturally independent of the tyrannies you seek to impose on us." A year earlier, Nicolas Negroponte, co-founder and director of MIT's Media Lab, flatly declared that "The Internet cannot be regulated," not because national "laws aren't relevant," but because "the nation-state is not relevant." Even economist and *New York Times* columnist Paul Krugman, writing in 2000, believed that the Internet represented a grave threat to copyright and tax laws because digital technology was "'erasing boundaries' and undermining government power."[56]

Connectivity and virtual statehood

For many, the Internet's role in the Arab Spring seemed to validate early visions of the Internet as a virtual global nation cum anti-state. As we will see in the next chapter, this view is influential but hardly universal. Still, those who hold the view can look back to People Power II in the Philippines and to other events for additionally validating precedents.

In 2004, for example, the Ukrainian presidential runoff election between Prime Minister Viktor Yanukovych, a throwback to the days in which Ukraine was a Soviet "republic," and democratic-leaning nationalist reformer Viktor Yushchenko gave Yanukovych the victory, although exit polls indicated that Yushchenko held a commanding lead. Even as state-controlled mass media reported the result as fact, digital media—the Internet and SMS texting—kept news concerning the discrepancy very much alive and flowing. As Volodymyr V. Lysenko and Kevin C. Desouza wrote in 2010, the Internet-based reports "proved to be decisive," provoking "indignation" among the Ukrainian people and "immediately [starting] mass protests."[57] Organization was facilitated by social media and mobile phones, and protestors took to wearing the orange clothing that gave the movement a compelling name: the "Orange Revolution." As Joshua Goldstein concluded in 2007, "the Internet allowed for the creation of a space for dissenting opinions of 'citizen journalists' in an otherwise self-censored media environment." The idea of "space" echoes the concept of "cyberspace" as a kind of parallel political universe in which thought can be freely expressed, unhindered by government control. In addition to this ideological function, Goldstein points out that the Internet—via mobile technology—played the tactical and logistical role of coordinating "a wide range of activities including election monitoring and large-scale protests."[58] "In retrospect," Philip Seib concludes, "the Orange Revolution may have been the first such event to have been organized primarily through the Internet."[59]

Of course, Americans don't have to look to the Philippines, the Middle East, or Ukraine for an example of Internet politics that may predict a coming age of cyberdiplomacy. The 2008 presidential campaign of Barack Obama stands as a stunning example of the effectiveness of social media even in mainstream politics. A Pew Internet & American Life Project report following the election, note that "46% of Americans have used the internet to get political news and share their thoughts about the campaign," "35 percent had watched online campaign videos," and "8 percent of Internet users (representing 6 percent of all adults) made a financial contribution to a candidate online."[60] By the numbers, it is clear that the Obama campaign used digital technology far more effectively than did the opposing campaign of Senator John McCain. As *USNews & World Report* reported in the tellingly titled "Barack Obama and the Facebook Election," Obama had 2 million+ U.S. supporters on Facebook versus 600,000+ for McCain. On Twitter, 112,000 supporters regularly tweeted, versus 4,600 for McCain. Obama supporters uploaded 1,800+ videos on Obama's YouTube channel, drawing 97 million views, whereas the McCain channel had 330 videos, attracting 25 million views.[61]

Of course, both the Obama and McCain campaigns spent prodigiously on broadcast television ads: $280 million for Obama, versus $134 million for McCain.[62] That the Obama campaign, praised for its social media savvy, outspent McCain on old-fashioned TV ads by more than 2 to 1 should serve as a corrective to those who predict that "traditional mass media will become less consequential" as social media continues to rise.[63] The fact is that, used skillfully, social media can leverage mass media and, for that matter, vice versa. Social media is not only an excellent platform for engaging interest in the issues of a campaign, it is a highly effective, efficient, and frictionless tool for soliciting and collecting financial contributions. This cash, in turn, finances mass media spending. In addition, while marketers universally agree that the most effective marketing is word of mouth, which social media can both generate and amplify, they also understand that nothing reinforces word of mouth more effectively than hearing it echoed and amplified by the mass media. This was demonstrated most dramatically in the 2016 presidential campaign, in which Hillary Clinton and super-PACS raised some $1.2 billion, spending $332.1 million on ads (mostly television), and Donald Trump raised $647 million, spending only $18.7 million on paid advertising (mostly television ads), but combining Twitter and live campaign rallies, which earned the former reality TV personality an estimated $2 billion in "earned" (i.e., free) television exposure. Trump's campaign also benefitted from other social media, ranging from support to the dissemination of "fake news" stories intended to undermine his opponent. These also generated broadcast news coverage of Trump's candidacy. For Trump, the synergy of digital and broadcast media was spectacularly effective.[64]

If government and diplomacy are to be augmented by social media to create networks among citizens, those networks will certainly benefit by the added presence of mass media. In revolutionary situations, decentralized social media have proven effective in countering and circumventing government-controlled mass media. This said, there is nothing more powerful than the convergence of the two electronic platforms. When the messages on social and mass media echo and reinforce one another, the impetus to believe becomes that much more compelling.

An end to insular diplomacy

At its inception, during 2010-2011, the Arab Spring inspired much speculation on the power of social media and mobile technology to create meaningful political and social change. The assessments, especially from Westerners, ranged from moderate, to hopeful, to rosy, to rhapsodic. As we will see in the next chapter, a significant minority critique, skeptical of the effect of the Internet in mass movements, has recently risen to counter the more positive narrative. Mostly, the critics point out that the technology of social media in and of itself is not sufficient to create meaningful political and social change. Some critics add that the unquestioning belief (again, prevalent among many Western commentators) that social media invariably nurtures democracy is both naïve and mistaken. A few point out that the Internet also serves organizations such as al-Qaeda and ISIS, among others—entities that are the very antithesis of secular democracy, as Westerners understand it.

"Al Qaeda," writes Philip Seib, "is a supranational network that relies on a mix of connectivity and geographical autonomy to accomplish its goals. Because of its relative permanence, Al Qaeda might be considered a mutation of a network, a 'virtual state.'"[65] Conventional diplomats have long referred to entities such as al-Qaeda and ISIS as "non-state actors." This may or may not have ever been a truly accurate designation. Or, more precisely, it was perhaps "accurate," but not very useful. In any case, with the social, religious, ideological, political, and tactical networking capabilities of the Internet developed to a high level of sophistication, the idea of a "non-state actor" may have become downright obsolete. To some degree, certainly, we have entered the era of the "virtual state," that is an entity relying on a mix of connectivity and geographical autonomy. Seib correctly implies that the US invasion of Afghanistan late in 2001, targeting the Taliban government for harboring al Qaeda and Osama bin Laden, was doomed to be at best minimally effective because "Afghanistan was not the Al Qaeda homeland .... The real Al Qaeda homeland is vast and virtual, given cohesion by using cyber tools and new media rather than by having territory defined by borders."[66]

At the very least, al-Qaeda's use of the Internet and mobile technology should prompt techno-romantics to acknowledge a dark side to cyber politics. It should also nudge traditional states and their diplomats into recognizing that they can no longer divide the world into inherently "legitimate" states and inherently "illegitimate" non-state actors. Digital connectivity may provide any sufficiently motivated group the technological means to create a "virtual state," which must, in some way be dealt with by the world's established states. Moreover, as the example of ISIS demonstrates, digital connectivity may allow a movement to become a virtual state, but if the constituents of that virtual state are sufficiently motivated and equipped, they can move credibly toward declaring themselves a state in a non-virtual dimension. Tune into any broadcast or cable news report, and you will, sooner or later, see a "map of ISIS"—a representation of the *physical* territory the entity controls, which it claims as the core of a religiously driven vision of a superstate, an empire known as the caliphate.

In traditional Islam, "the caliphate" is a hybrid of political-religious leadership focused on the *caliph*—that is, the "successor" to the prophet Muhammad. In more abstract or conceptual terms, the caliphate is the sovereign state of all Islam, known as the Ummah, and it both crosses and transcends states that are defined by political borders. Traditionally, the cohesion of the Ummah is derived from the shared faith of the Muslim people. ISIS, however, enforces this religious cohesion with the brutal terror of military conquest. The results, so far, have been horrific and have instilled fear far beyond the Middle East. This said, insofar as ISIS may manage to make a transition from virtual state—an entity sustainable at least in some degree by the Internet—to actual (albeit terrorist) state, it will inevitably sacrifice the advantages of a "vast and virtual homeland." The sacrifice might well render it vulnerable to the long-familiar tools of conventional diplomacy, ranging from the economic and political sanctions of a global community to military action by a formidable coalition of established states. As of 2017, however, the physical territory controlled or occupied by ISIS has shrunk radically, and the organization seems to have turned increasingly to the Internet to incite so-called homegrown acts of terrorism, especially in Europe and the United States. Whereas as al-Qaeda used the Internet and the social web to recruit fighters to come to bases in the Middle East and elsewhere for training, ISIS used these media to inspire people to commit acts of terrorism wherever they happened to live.[67]

However ISIS may wax or wane in the non-virtual realm, it is clear that nation-states will increasingly have to incorporate the Internet and its apparatus into the formulation and execution of their global public policies. The world wars and Cold War of the twentieth century proved that diplomats could no longer rely exclusively on talking exclusively to designated officials or to a select handful of influential people. In the last century, propaganda emerged as the leading vehicle of what came to be called public diplomacy. During the Cold War years, the US funded Radio Free Europe and the Voice of America to broadcast the message of democracy through the so-called Iron Curtain. In 2011, the Voice of America officially shut down its shortwave broadcast service to the People's Republic of China and instead funded digital technology. In a blog posted on *One Jerusalem*, the Israeli diplomat who created Israel's official government blog in 2006 and encouraged the creation of IsraelPolitik.org, David Saranga, wrote that "social networks ... have become tools that allow us to spread Israel's message directly—unmediated by the press. Furthermore, our messages can be spread not only by the Government of Israel but also by our supporters around the world for whom it is important—and rightfully so—to give the Israeli narrative worldwide attention." He explained that "Israeli government officials have achieved success by becoming the first governmental body in the world to use new media tools to create public discourse while passing along Israel's narrative."[68] Saranga's outreach not only used blogs and Internet forums, but also Twitter, via a "Citizens Press Conference," by which anyone could post questions directly to representatives of the government. For instance: "Israeli Consul David Saranga (NYC) answers ur questions in a citizens 'press' conference, Tue Dec 30, 1-3 pm EST #AskIsrael #gaza #sderot."[69] The US Department of State created a Digital Outreach Team and program in 2011 and achieved what Philip Seib characterizes as "mixed results," largely due to the requirement that anything diplomats post online must first be reviewed by colleagues. The review process typically delays each post by nearly three days, making true "real-time" public diplomacy difficult.[70]

Seib's assessment in 2012 holds true today: "Diplomats are still grappling with ways to use networks without being overwhelmed by the participatory intensity they can engender."[71] In the meantime, activists such as Ramy Raoof, have compiled and posted suggestions for how individuals who "are participating in a peaceful assembly as a [*sic*] journalists, rights defender, or activists" can use their mobile phones "to communicate with allies, to document the events, and [to] bear witness to what is happening around you."[72] Such instructions tend to run counter to Seib's conclusion that "Foreign policy does not lend itself to crowdsourcing."[73] Yet Seib also concedes that the "insular world that diplomats for so long inhabited and controlled cannot survive amidst thriving popular networks."[74] To fully embrace crowdsourced diplomacy would be to abrogate the last vestiges of the traditional nation-state in global relations. This will not happen. Yet neither can diplomats remain "insular" and aloof from the crowd. Citizen and other private sector networks have always existed. By enabling or facilitating connectivity, the Internet has both expanded and multiplied them, has increased their access to information, and has accelerated their ability to respond to events and the actions of governments. The digitized networks make demands of the government. These cannot simply be ignored. In addition, these same networks offer the government data relating to public sentiment and present a variety of ideas about problems as well as solutions. As such, they shape political action as well as reportage. For these reasons as well, the networks cannot be ignored by those responsible for creating public policy, both domestically and globally. People Power 2.0 is not confined to uprising and revolution. It is an aspect—a large and growing aspect—of community, nationhood, and global society in times of relative normality as well as intense stress.

CHAPTER 3
THE EMPIRES STRIKE BACK

On the morning of June 13, 2009, the Islamic Republic News Agency, official media organ of the Iranian government, projected incumbent president Mahmoud Ahmadinejad the victor in the nation's tenth presidential election. After two-thirds of the ballots were counted, the incumbent was ahead with 62 percent of the votes. Independent Reformist candidate Mir-Hossein Mousavi, the runner-up in a field of four contenders, had captured 34 percent, according to the agency.

What Western governments and media, as well as Mousavi supporters, characterized as "irregularities"—violence preceding the election, mobile phone interruptions and possible jamming on election day, and allegations of widespread vote rigging—triggered protests by millions of Iranians in every Iranian city and across the world. These demonstrations, riots, and acts of civil disobedience extended over eight months and, by Iranians, have been variously called the Green Revolution, the Green Wave, and the Sea of Green Persian Awakening (after the color initially adopted by the Mousavi campaign). By non-Iranians—mostly Westerners—the movement was called the Facebook Revolution or, even more frequently, the Twitter Revolution.

The latter name gained currency after political commentator Andrew Sullivan published a blog titled "The Revolution Will Be Twittered" in *The Atlantic.*[75] As Evgeny Morozov noted in *The Net Delusion: The Dark Side of Internet Freedom,* Sullivan's blog "emerged as a major information hub that provided almost instantaneous links to Iran-related developments." Sullivan captured many eyeballs online, and Morozov commented) it "didn't take long for [his] version of events to gain hold elsewhere in the blogosphere."[76] Since, by 2009, traditional broadcast, cable, and print media had begun relying heavily on the Internet for much that it reported, Sullivan's impression that Twitter and Facebook were fomenting, driving, organizing, and sustaining the revolution was widely reported as simple fact. Another *Atlantic* writer, Marc Ambinder, wrote, "When histories of the Iranian election are written, Twitter will doubtless be cast as a protagonal [*sic*] technology that enabled the powerless to survive a brutal crackdown and information blackout by the ruling authorities."[77] Conservative blogger Ross Kaminsky proclaimed that Twitter had accomplished what "neither the U.N. nor the European Union have been able to do" and "what the Great Satan [an Iranian pejorative for the United States] is too preoccupied with its finances to even try," namely incite a rebellion against the hardcore Islamist government of Iran.[78] On the other side of the American political spectrum, NPR commentator Daniel Schorr, a mainstream liberal, proclaimed that "in Iran, tyranny has run afoul of technology in the form of the Internet, turning a protest into a movement," and Nicholas Kristof, in *The New York Times,* put "government thugs firing bullets" and "young protesters firing 'tweets'" on opposing sides of what he characterized as "the quintessential 21st-century conflict."[79] Clay Shirky, the well-respected writer on the socioeconomic effects of the Internet, called the Iranian protest "the first revolution that has been catapulted onto a global stage and transformed by social media."[80]

Nor were bloggers, journalists, and Internet gurus the only onlookers who ascribed to Twitter (and other social media) a kind of omnipotence. Mark Pfeifle, ex-deputy national security advisor to George W. Bush, headed up a campaign to secure Twitter's nomination for a Nobel Peace Prize. He argued that, "without Twitter, the people of Iran would not have felt empowered and confident to stand up for freedom and democracy."[81] In other words, social media did not merely aid and facilitate revolution, it was indispensable to it because Iranians would have been too feeble to challenge Ahmadinejad without this product of Western technology.

Faulty logic

To give him his due, Mark Pfeifle intended to praise Twitter, not to bury Iranian activists. In his assessment of the sovereign potency of social media, a force that apparently made individual human activists superfluous, Pfeifle was outdone by no less a figure than the prime minister of the United Kingdom, Gordon Brown. Thanks to Twitter and the like, Brown declared, "You cannot have Rwanda again because information would come out far more quickly about what is actually going on and public opinion would grow to the point where action would need to be taken."[82] Both Pfeifle and Brown made explicit what the bloggers and journalists only implied—that Internet technology is not merely a tool of revolution, it is also revolution's agent, cause, and sustainer. In this view, activists—revolutionaries—are not the creators of social change, but the creators of content to drive the *real* creator, namely the technology of social media. It is a position that is perilously analogous to attributing the American Revolution to the ringing of the Liberty Bell.

Morozov calls the view that attributes social change to Internet technology rather than to dedicated activists *using* Internet technology among other tactics and strategies "Internet-centrism." For him, Internet-centrism is, in turn, a product of "cyber-utopianism."[83] Cyber-utopianism may itself be understood as the most recent manifestation of the kind of technological utopianism that characterized everything from "classic" science fiction to the philosophy of Henry Ford, R. Buckminster Fuller, and even Edward Teller—the "father" of the hydrogen bomb and the godfather of the "Atoms for Peace" initiative launched by President Dwight D. Eisenhower at the end of 1953.[84] Technological utopianism has driven a great many large-scale commercial enterprise since the twentieth century and was at the heart of "world's fairs" and other international industrial expositions beginning with the 1844 French Industrial Exposition in Paris and the "Great Exhibition" held in London's Crystal Palace in 1851 and culminating in the world's fairs staged between 1939 and 1987.

Proponents tend to present the chief premise of technological utopianism as self-evident, namely that technology inevitably improves life and civilization. Positions counter to this are regarded as a minority viewpoint, typically the work of literary types with an intellectual axe to grind—the likes of Karel čapek (*R.U.R.*), Aldous Huxley (*Strange New World*), George Orwell (*1984*), and others who cast technology as an instrument of oppression. Those who question the intellectual, philosophical, sociological, and historical assumptions behind the subset of technological utopianism Morozov dubbed cyber-utopianism constitute an even smaller minority. For that reason, proposing that Twitter be awarded a Nobel Peace Prize elicited neither widespread dissent nor derision. To most it seemed a plausible prospect and maybe even a good idea.

Those who do persist in questioning the omnipotence of the Internet are not luddites. On the contrary, they tend to be technologically savvy, often, in fact, technologists. They believe that Internet technology is, on balance, a remarkable boon for civilization and humankind. What concerns them, however, is the absence of critical thought that should accompany the application of this technology to influence governments and public policy and to organize political and social movements, including those of protest and revolt.

Matters of fact

Western media and Western diplomats were not the only believers in the apparently boundless power of the Internet to create democratic revolution. In 2010, the Iranian government itself accused U.S.-based CNN of training hackers to sabotage pro-Ahmadinejad websites, while Iranian pro-Ahmadinejad media accused the U.S. State Department of employing Twitter to foment outright rebellion.[85]

Those Westerners with a candid view of history might scoff at the idea of CNN training hackers, but would have to acknowledge that the United States government did have a record of covertly intervening in Iranian affairs. In 1953, the CIA was instrumental in triggering a successful coup against the nationalist and anti-Western government of Mohammad Mosaddegh. That America would now use U.S.-based Twitter against Ahmadinejad was, understandably, far from implausible to most Iranians. When anti-Ahmadinejad Iranian activists used Twitter to protest the results of the 2009 election, a senior U.S. State Department official sent an email to Twitter executives asking that they postpone a scheduled maintenance shutdown of the Twitter website so as not to disrupt the protest. The executives complied, but publicly announced that they did so not at the request of the State Department but out of their own sense that Twitter was serving an important purpose in the course of world affairs. *The New York Times* did not take Twitter's disclaimer at face value and instead called the State Department intervention a "new-media milestone" for the Obama administration, ascribing to the U.S. government the belief that Twitter "has the potential to change history in an ancient Islamic country."[86]

Suddenly, Iranian Twitter users were branded as the vanguard of U.S.-led revolution. What is more, Chinese officials seized on the State Department email to Twitter as an indication that the United States was launching a digital offensive using U.S. high-tech companies to ignite revolutions not only in Iran, but in China and elsewhere, including youth protests in Moldava in April 2010. *China National Defense,* an official periodical of the Chinese military, spoke of the Internet as a weapon in America's "diplomatic arsenal." The publication called for additional government control of China's Internet to prevent its "becoming a new poisoned arrow for hostile forces."[87]

Did the Chinese government really believe Twitter was so powerful? Or did it simply seize upon a *New York Times* story that reported the State Department's apparent belief in the power of Twitter in order to bolster and justify a call for tighter control over digital freedom? In either case, the result was far from what the Obama administration wanted. Instead of promoting Internet freedom and thereby enhancing a purported democratizing technology, the episode provided an excuse for a digital crackdown by authoritarian regimes in Iran, China, and, potentially, other places.

In and of itself, this result was ironic. But the irony went even deeper than was initially apparent.

The United States publicly criticized the Iranian government for rounding up bloggers. In all candor, the U.S. Department of State should also have criticized itself for openly requesting that Twitter hold off on a service interruption. After all, the only reasonable interpretation of this request was that, in the eyes of the U.S. government, Twitter was crucial to fomenting unrest—even revolution—in Iran. Why else send the email?

So, at least on the face of it, the governments of both Iran and the United States seemed to be in perfect agreement: Twitter was starting an uprising.

Yet the fact is—and this is the deepest irony of all—both governments were acting not on sophisticated intelligence concerning the actual presence and effect of Twitter, but on Western media stories and mere assumptions by Western policymakers. Both the media and cyber-utopianists within the U.S. government blithely asserted that the revolution was being tweeted. Yet at least two significant factual unknowns exist concerning Twitter in Iran in 2009-2010. First, no one knows how many people *within the country* were tweeting about the protests. Second, while pundits claimed that Twitter was key to organizing and directing the protests, there is no hard evidence—*from the inside*—that this was indeed the case.[88]

While the volume of tweets relating to Iran was high during the two weeks after the suspect election, given the borderless nature of these messages, it is impossible to locate them geographically. That is, to this day, we do not know how many of the tweets came from inside Iran and how many from outside, especially from the extensive Iranian diaspora—virtually all of which can be assumed to oppose the Ahmadinejad government. The social media analytical company Sysomos concluded that only 19,235 Twitter accounts were actually registered inside of Iran on the eve of the 2009 elections. This represents a mere 0.027 percent of the Iranian population.[89] It is also known that many expatriate supporters of the anti-Ahmadinejad movement deliberately changed their Twitter location status to Tehran in an effort to confound Iranian authorities. Indeed, Al-Jazeera's director of new media, Moeed Ahmad, reported in

2010 that his fact checkers could confirm just sixty Twitter accounts in all of Tehran. To be sure, Iran-related tweets were plentiful during the early weeks of election protests, but the "vast majority of them were not authored or retweeted by those in Iran."[90] They were news pieces and comments, not on-the-spot reports or tactical items intended to direct protest. In short, while Twitter was ablaze during the Iranian protests, it seems not to have been geographically, strategically, or tactically at the heart of anything approaching a revolution.

One "prominent Iranian blogger" went so far as to report, "Twitter never became very popular in Iran." The impression that it was popular was an illusion: "because the world was watching Iran … during those days, it led many to believe falsely that Iranian people were also getting their news through Twitter." As for Twitter's role in organizing the protest, those who took part in it complain that the protest was hardly organized at all. Alireza Rezaei, another Iranian blogger, remarked that the movement was "reactive"—responding to unfolding events—rather than coordinated by any centralized decisions transmitted to others. Even more significantly, Hamid Tehrani, Persian editor of the Global Voices blogging network, called the label "Twitter Revolution" a Western invention and observed that the "west was focused not on the Iranian people but on the role of western technology." The manager of *Balatarin,* a Farsi-language news website based in Los Angeles, believed that "Twitter's impact inside Iran is zero."[91]

Or maybe not zero. An Iranian correspondent for Radio Free Europe, Glonaz Esfandiari, saw Twitter as having a negative impact on post-election events because of its "pernicious complicity in allowing rumors to spread," including one that police helicopters were pouring acid and boiling water on protestors.[92]

Critics like Morozov conclude that the so-called Twitter Revolution in Iran belongs on "the gigantic pile of other urban myths about the Internet's mighty potential to topple dictators."[93] Even the distinguished *Guardian* newspaper published in early 2010 an op ed by Oxford University doctoral candidate Reza Zia-Ebrahimi calling for the Western democracies to "bombard Iran … with broadband," providing Iranians with free satellite Internet access in a digital connectivity offensive that would "allow the Iranian citizen-journalists to wider circulate images and videos of government violence, and coordinate more efficiently their demonstrations."[94] Two remarkable—and, it turns out, insupportable—assumptions are implicit in this recommendation. First: the Internet is a virtual weapon more effective than any actual "kinetic" weapons. Second: Give the people enough Internet access and they not only can but will—almost inevitably—topple the regime that oppresses them.

What happens after the brass lamp is rubbed?

The rise of the Internet has been so rapid and widespread as to have taken many of society's arbiters by storm. Politicians, diplomats, activists, world leaders, media commentators, and technologists have tended to interpret the social, political, and economic effects of the Internet uncritically. It is not simply that they attribute to it godlike powers, but that, in so doing, they typically commit a fundamental error in logic. There can be no doubt that Internet technology has been transformative. It would be foolish to deny that it has and will continue to have profound effects on society and civilization at the local, national, and global levels. However, many of those charged with shaping and interpreting social and political policy have often mistaken the technology—*tools* and *media*—that facilitates social and political change for the *agent* of change.

Some years ago in America, the National Rifle Association (NRA) responded to calls for gun control with a bumper sticker proclaiming, "Guns Don't Kill People. People Kill People." Like all bumper sticker slogans devoted to complex issues, it begged to be mocked, and gun control advocates universally mocked it. Yet there is an undeniable core of logic in this slogan. However laudable or harmful its message, the bumper sticker does embody the virtue of recognizing that people, not technology, are the agents of action and behavior. It is this very basic recognition that is often missing from evaluations of the role of the Internet in driving social and political change and even in fomenting, organizing, and sustaining revolution. People, not technology, are the agents of change. *They* must desire it and create it. This requires, among other things, imagination, will, passion, persuasive force, and courage. Technology, in contrast, neither desires nor creates. It neither possesses nor supplies imagination, will, passion, persuasive force, or courage.

The metaphor of the genie released from the bottle and put at the command of whoever rubbed that vessel has been applied so often to the Internet as to be both trivial and tiresome. Yet, for all that, it is not an entirely inappropriate metaphor—especially if we trouble ourselves to go beneath the superficial shell of cliché by interrogating the metaphor. We need to ask: *What happens after the brass lamp is rubbed?*

The Western concept of the genie is derived from the *jinn,* a supernatural creature found both in Islamic mythology and in Arabian mythology before the advent of Islam. In Western popular culture, drawing on various translations of folktales originally compiled in Arabic during the so-called Golden Age of Islam (eighth century through the mid-thirteenth century), the genie is typically depicted as a powerful spirit trapped in a kind of brass oil lamp. When the human finder of the lamp happens to rub it, the genie is released and rewards his liberator with a promise to grant three wishes. Over the years, this trope has produced many stories—tales, poems, books, movies, TV shows, and so on. Most share a common theme of granted wishes that produce disastrous results. Sometimes, the disaster is a case of unintended consequences. Most often, however, it results from the flawed or foolish nature of the wishes themselves.

None of us needs a lecture on the potential of the Internet as a means of accessing seemingly limitless troves of information and knowledge, of real-time and close-to-real-time news, of entertainment, of communications, and of virtually frictionless commerce. Those of us born before the emergence of the Internet, all readily remark on the myriad ways in which the technology has transformed our lives. And yet no Internet meme is more pervasive than the cute cat video. Among all the potential profundities into which it may admit us, the Internet has become inextricably associated with nothing more profound than the cute cat video. No wonder. As of late October 2014, YouTube had about 2 million cat video postings, which had produced, collectively, 25 billion views.[95] The genie can grant our greatest wishes. When it pops out of the lamp, however, many of us ask for something—well, not so much stupid or bad or disastrous, but merely trivial.

On January 21, 2010, then Secretary of State Hillary Clinton spoke at the Newseum in Washington, D.C., on the subject of "Internet Freedom." The speech has been widely praised, as it should be. Unlike some, who take an uncritical utopian view of the Internet, Clinton acknowledged, first, that Internet "technologies are not an unmitigated blessing."

> These tools are also being exploited to undermine human progress and political rights. Just as steel can be used to build hospitals or machine guns, or nuclear power can either energize a city or destroy it, modern information networks and the technologies they support can be harnessed for good or for ill. The same networks that help organize movements for freedom also enable al-Qaida to spew hatred and incite violence against the innocent. And technologies with the potential to open up access to government and promote transparency can also be hijacked by governments to crush dissent and deny human rights.

Second, she carefully distinguished between *tool* and *agent,* observing. "On their own, new technologies do not take sides in the struggle for freedom and progress …"[96]

After these important nods to reality, Secretary Clinton extolled the Internet as the "freedom to connect" and compared it to the "freedom of assembly, only in cyberspace." She spoke of how the Internet allowed "individuals to get online, come together, and hopefully cooperate."[97] These are laudable expressions of the Internet's potential for enabling social and political change. But are they realistic? Do people—even "oppressed" people—use the Internet as a public square and townhall? Evgeny Morozov answers by pointing out that Russia.ru, "Russia's pioneering experiment in Internet television supported by Kremlin's ideologues," does produce a handful of shows that discuss politics, but most of the fare it offers is "quite frivolous in nature." His case in point is *The Tits Show*, about a "horny and slightly overweight young man [who] travels around Moscow nightclubs in search of perfect breasts."[98]

Whether it's a quest for the cutest cat videos or the perfect breasts, there is an argument to be made that vast tracts of the Internet merit the very label FCC chairman Newton Minow applied to television in his famous May 9, 1961 address to the convention of the National Association of Broadcasters: "I invite each of you to sit down in front of your own television set when your station goes on the air and stay there, for a day, without a book, without a magazine, without a newspaper, without a profit and loss sheet or a rating book to distract you. Keep your eyes glued to that set until the station signs off. I can assure you that what you will observe is a *vast wasteland*" (italics added).[99]   Far from serving as cyberspace townhall, a virtual forum in which the people can debate, create, and drive needed change, the Internet often serves as a weapon not of mass destruction but of mass distraction. It has been compared to the mass-produced pornography the state churns out to keep the "proles" complacent in George Orwell's *1984*. It may even be seen as the digital equivalent of Karl Marx's description of religion, as the "opium of the people" (*"Opium des Volkes"*).

At the very least, there is no guarantee that any given individual will use the Internet wisely, and it is even less certain that any given democratic political group will use it effectively. Secretary of State Clinton told her Newseum audience, "Once you're on the internet, you don't need to be a tycoon or a rock star to have a huge impact on society."[100] Although this is one of those utterances that, these days, comes across as a truism, it is patently untrue. At any moment, hundreds of thousands or even millions of Internet users are tweeting or posting this or that opinion. How many eyes actually encounter any one of these? On a platform in which anyone can make noise, few noisemakers will actually be heard, let alone heeded. In theory, access to the Internet gives any individual a global audience. In practice, access does no such thing.

The audience simply does not tune in. If a tree falls in the forest …

Presumptuous assumptions

Secretary Clinton's pseudo-truism, that the Internet can give anyone the impact of a rock star or a tycoon, calls to mind another. Clinton and others argue that free access to the Internet is important because, given free and unbiased access to information, people will inevitably choose truth over lies, freedom over oppression, and democracy over authoritarianism. As Thomas Friedman wrote in *The Lexus and the Olive Tree: Understanding Globalization,* "In a few years"—thanks to unfettered access to the Internet—"every citizen of the world will be able to comparison shop between his own country and his own government and the one next door."[101] The assumption is that, having done so, the citizen will inevitably choose Western democracy. From this assumption, we can leap to the implication that it is therefore imperative for Western democracies to do whatever they can to bring free and uncensored Internet access to every corner of the globe.

Let us concede that everything in the preceding paragraph is appealing and has the ring of plausibility about it. Neither of these qualities, however, makes the paragraph true.

To begin with, there is an assumption that the West possesses *all* of the truth, freedom, and democracy. The assumption is presumptuous at best and unwarranted at worst. Next, the assertion that, if only informed and empowered, people will necessarily choose truth, freedom, and democracy is an assumption passed off as self-evident fact. Many people in many places and during much of history have—in fact—chosen a comfortable status quo of stable authoritarianism over the risky prospect of democratic change. For many, the sternest kind of theocracy provides spiritual assurances that seem to them far more important than, say, freedom of expression. While those of us in the Western democracies purport to believe that the only legitimate government is that created by, of, and for the people, many elsewhere do not equate legitimacy with popular election.

In the 1920s, the overwhelming majority of Italians embraced the often brutal authoritarianism of Benito Mussolini as preferable to the chaotic and impoverished "freedom" democracy had brought to Germany's Weimar Republic. Mussolini "has not only been able to secure and hold an almost universal following; he has built a new state upon a new concept of a state. He has not only been able to change the lives of human beings but he has changed their minds, their hearts, their spirits. He has not merely ruled a house; he has built a new house. … It is one thing to administer a state. The one who does this well is called statesman. It is quite another thing to make a state. Mussolini has made a state. That is superstatesmanship." This assessment came not from a member of the Italian Fascist Party or even from an Italian of the period, but from Richard Washburn Child, who had served in the early 1920s as the United States ambassador to Italy. He wrote it in the foreword to the autobiography he proudly claimed credit for having persuaded Mussolini to write. "For his autobiography I am responsible," Child crowed, and, like so many of us, he took delight in having recognized greatness and celebrity from the beginning, before almost anyone else: "I knew him before the world at large, outside of Italy, had ever heard of him; I knew him before and after the moment he leaped into the saddle and in the days when he, almost single-handed, was clearing away chaos' own junk pile from Italy."[102]

Today, Chinese who enjoy unprecedented prosperity do not universally clamor for democracy. Russians who feel renewed pride in nationalism do not universally criticize Vladimir Putin for failing to be Abraham Lincoln. The people of Singapore do not universally complain about a plethora of restrictive rules of conduct when they enjoy a high degree of commercial prosperity and an abundance of government services.

Friedman implies that the Internet, by providing the opportunity to "comparison shop" among governments and ways of life, will perforce doom all dictatorships. Assuming this degree of Internet access reaches them, will the Chinese, Russians, and Singaporeans give up the perceived benefits they now enjoy to embrace the uncertainties of democracy? Perhaps. Perhaps not. The availability of information does not necessarily mean people will access it, and, even if they do, that they will necessarily act upon it.

Liberation technology, or just technology?

At its best, the Internet can be a *tool* for political and diplomatic action and change. Even at its best, however, the Internet cannot be an *agent* of change. Technology can be a tool, but agency requires human thought, desire, will, courage, and action. These human qualities do exist and have figured in every significant political and social movement, including those in which Internet technology has played a demonstrable role. It is also true, however, that, for most people most of the time, the Internet is a recreation and a distraction. It is, like so much entertainment throughout history, an anodyne.

Well, we all need relief, and, in the best cases, a suitable anodyne like the Internet is beneficial or, at least, harmless. In the worst cases, however, where government is oppressive, the Internet may well serve as the opium of the people, Orwell's mass-produced porn that keeps the proles complacent. This use of a new technology is as old as the "bread and circuses" Juvenal wrote of circa AD 100 (in *Satires*, 10:81) in lambasting what he regarded as the complacent egocentrism of the masses.

But the new technology can do far worse than merely soothe, placate, distract, and appease. As we have seen in chapter 2, there is a widespread assumption that the Internet, by connecting people with people even in defiance of their governments, is inevitably a force for good. On February 8, 1996, Electronic Frontier Foundation founding member (and sometime Grateful Dead lyricist) John Perry Barlow published "A Declaration of the Independence of Cyberspace," which begins: "Governments of the Industrial World, you weary giants of flesh and steel, I come from Cyberspace, the new home of Mind. On behalf of the future, I ask you of the past to leave us alone. You are not welcome among us. You have no sovereignty where we gather ... I declare the global social space we are building to be naturally independent of the tyrannies you seek to impose on us."[103] A year earlier, Nicolas Negroponte, co-founder and director of MIT's Media Lab, had flatly declared that the Internet was beyond the reach of national laws, not because these "laws aren't relevant," but because "the nation-state is not relevant."[104] To many, the Arab Spring and other popular movements—such as "People Power II" in the Philippines (2001), the "Orange Revolution" in Ukraine (2004), and the first Obama presidential campaign (2008)—seemed obvious vindication of Barlow and other early techno-romantics.

Acting on the assumption that free and unfettered Internet access can do nothing but good—that the Internet is, in the phrase of Larry Diamond (Hoover Institution fellow and director of Stanford's Center on Democracy, Development, and the Rule of Law), a "liberation technology"[105]—Austin Heap, a twenty-five-year-old programmer living in San Francisco, suddenly became passionately interested in Iran's election protest. He told *Newsweek* that, in June 2009, he read about what was happening in Iran and "decided to become involved in a battle more than 7,000 miles away in a country he admits he knew nest to nothing about. 'I remember literally saying, "OK, game on.'"[106]

Heap set about creating a program that activists could use to circumvent Iranian cyber surveillance and Internet censorship. He called it Haystack (as in something that makes finding a needle difficult) and soon attracted the notice of BBC TV's *Virtual Revolution* series, which promoted it as a cutting-edge means of bypassing network blocking software. In fact, it was claimed that the Heap's app not only could penetrate government firewalls but would also function as a proxy that effectively masked the Web surfing of its users.

Beta versions of Haystack were distributed, and Heap drew increasing media attention, *The Guardian* even proclaiming him "Innovator of the Year" in March 2010.[107] While reporters and politicians greeted Haystack uncritically, many in the technology community became skeptical, arguing that it was far from secure. On September 13, 2010, *The Washington Post* reported that user testing of Haystack had been abruptly halted because testing by independent third-party experts revealed that the program was dangerous. Far from disguising the identity of users, it made it easy for government monitors to trace them.[108] In a blog posted on *ComputerworldUK*, Simon Phipps was even more direct, claiming that "The naïve enthusiasm of an American marketing graduate, hyped by the world media, may have risked the lives of Iranian activists through over-reaching claims for an inadequately understood software system."[109] Haystack was soon shut down—permanently.

Haystack is an extreme but highly illustrative example of the consequences of uncritical reliance on Internet technology as "liberation technology," an unalloyed force for good. The app was created with the best of intentions—by a marketing-oriented programmer whose understanding of conditions in Iran was superficial at best, in terms of its society, politics, government, *and* that government's technological capabilities. The creation of Haystack failed to contemplate the possibility that Iranian authorities could and would turn the program against its users. In the end, Haystack was the work of a poorly informed Westerner who believed he could contribute something to the creation of democracy in a distant nation and among a people of whom he knew virtually nothing.

Fortunately, perhaps only a dozen or so Iranian users actually tested Haystack, and there is no evidence that any of them was, as a result, actually traced by Iranian authorities or came to any harm due to their use of the program. Hyped and failed, Haystack is nevertheless valuable for the lesson it teaches: "Liberation technology" is first and foremost *technology,* period. In and of itself, it is morally neutral. Like a hammer, it can be used to build a house or to bludgeon a victim, depending on the human agent who wields it.

To his credit, Larry Diamond, while optimistic about Internet technology as a liberation technology, did not claim the Internet as a silver bullet against tyranny and oppression or as a technology that invariably produces salutary results. Consider his discussion of the March 2003 case of Sun Zhigang, whom the police detained because of his inability to produce on demand a "temporary living permit," required of citizens moving from some jurisdictions to others. After three days in police custody, Sun died. When officials attributed the death of this twenty-seven year old to a heart attack, his parents authorized an autopsy, which revealed that he had been brutally beaten. The entire incident was reported in a local newspaper and was subsequently picked up by national media and the Web, which triggered an explosion of "outrage" on Internet chat rooms and bulletin boards throughout China. The central government soon had no choice but to launch an official investigation, which found twelve local officials complicit in Sun's death. Diamond points out that, in this instance, not only did Internet activism force investigation and prosecution of official wrongdoing, it provoked a national debate on the Custody and Repatriation (C&R) "measures that allowed the police to detain rural migrants … for lacking a residency or temporary-living permit." In the wake of the incident, many "Chinese citizens posted on the Internet stories of their own experiences of C&R" and "in June 200s the government announced it would close all of the more than eight-hundred C&R detention centers."[110]

Diamond commented that "optimists" see the string of events triggered by Sun's death as evidence of the "striking ability of the Internet … to empower individuals, facilitate interdependent communication and mobilization, and strengthen emergent civil society." But he also pointed out that "pessimists" accurately claim that "nothing in China … fundamentally changed" as a result of the Internet-facilitated activism. Not only did the Chinese Communist Party remain firmly in control, the "Chinese state has developed an unparalleled system of digital censorship." On balance, both the optimist and pessimist points of view, Diamond concluded, "have merit." He observed that "liberation technology enables citizens to report news, expose wrongdoing, express opinions, mobilize protest, monitor elections, scrutinize government, deepen participation, and expand the horizons of freedom," yet numerous "authoritarian states … have acquired (and shared) impressive technical capabilities to filter and control the Internet, and to identify and punish dissenters." He judged that "democrats and autocrats" were in competition "to master these technologies." More importantly, Diamond concluded that "not just technology but political organization and strategy and deep-rooted normative, social, and economic forces will determine who 'wins' the race." Mastery of technology is less decisive than human action and institutions.[111]

In the meantime, applications such as GreenDam—for a time required to be installed on all computers in China—employ predictive censorship to analyze a user's browsing and other computer behavior to anticipate certain proscribed online activities and preemptively and dynamically intervene. Reportedly, for example, if GreenDam detects an excessive amount of pink in photos a user is viewing online, it assumes that illegal pornography is being accessed and responds by shutting down the photo-viewing app. GreenDam reports on user behavior, so that it functions not only to block access to objectionable sites, but also to monitor attempts to access them. Originally deployed in 2009, GreenDam was so heavy handed that it was subsequently withdrawn. But its existence suggests that subtler and more sophisticated preemptive filtering software may well be in the offing.

Not that authoritarian states want simply to block everything. Many, for example, actually encourage membership on facebook and other social websites, which then become a treasure trove of volunteered personal information. State security operatives routinely comb facebook to identify potential dissidents and to monitor those already identified. The social web can be a boon to state surveillance.

As for blogging, most authoritarian regimes have taken a sharply strategic rather than a bluntly restrictive approach. Most tolerate a certain amount of blogging that is critical of the government or aspects of the government, presumably to convey the impression of a degree of liberalization. The presence of some dissidence suggests that the government has nothing to hide and is tolerant of free expression. At the same time, a number of governments, including those of the People's Republic of China and Russia, encourage blogging by pro-government individuals. In some cases, such bloggers are either openly or covertly employed by the government. But the fact is that nationalism and a desire for law, order, and security motivate many bloggers to express enthusiasm for the ostensibly undemocratic policies of their government. Indeed, government-sponsored social media campaigns often crowdsource censorship and monitoring, soliciting their citizens to report pornography and other illegal content—including politically objectionable websites and blogs—when they encounter it. No reward is offered. The sole motivation of these volunteer digital monitors/stool pigeons appears to be a feeling of solidarity with the government and its policies.

Even an episode such as the response to the beating death of Sun Zhigang may be seen as an example of what some call the "Spinternet," a regime's use of the Internet to "spin" information and disseminate propaganda. The Spinternet approach eschews censorship—the outright blocking of websites—and instead seeks to flood the Internet with "spun" material that conveys or reinforces a desired ideological message or "party line." The vigorous investigation and prosecution of the officials who abused and ultimately killed Sun Zhigang may be seen as a way of spinning an instance of government corruption and brutality into an instance of government responsiveness to a popular demand for justice. The people Diamond calls pessimists would see this as a way of admitting fault and offering a remedy while all the while preserving the status quo of an authoritarian regime.

Nor are all anti-democratic uses of the Internet the product of oppressive central governments. Westerners especially tend to view the Internet as a global phenomenon capable of transcending national borders and even of rendering national, regional, ethnic, and religious identity more or less obsolescent. It is popularly believed that the Internet knows no borders and recognizes no political or cultural distinctions. In fact, however, as digital marketers keenly realize, one of the great strengths of the Internet is that it allows the customization and personalization of information. By definition, traditional non-interactive mass broadcast media can offer very little customization. Its business model is such that it must appeal to the lowest common denominator to reach the largest possible audience. The Internet, on the contrary, despite its potential for global reach, can deliver information and "programming" targeted at very specific audience sectors, all the way down to the specific individual. Amazon and other sophisticated online merchants continually send us advertisements tailored to our buying habits and personal interests as revealed by the websites we browse and the merchandise we look at or purchase online. Governments likewise appeal to narrow nationalism, narrow religious affiliations, narrow ethnic communities, and other shared values to segment and divide the world rather than to unite it. Often, the message is not "We are the world," but "It is us against the world." While some continue to insist that the Internet is a boon to globalism, others point out that it has almost certainly done even more to facilitate nationalism and religious extremism. One has only to consider the slick sophistication of recruiting and fund-raising websites belonging to the likes of al-Qaeda and ISIS.

Hardwired reality

As we saw in chapter 2, before the news out of the Middle East turned almost universally terrible, many Westerners were wide-eyed over the Arab Spring. Technologists, especially those in and around Silicon Valley, were quick to attribute the Middle Eastern uprisings that began in 2010 to a combination of social media and mobile phones. Clay Shirky wrote of digital technology having created in the Middle East a "networked population" that, thanks to the Internet, enjoyed "more opportunities to engage in public speech ... and ... undertake collective action."[112]

The popular movements in Tunisia and Egypt were blithely dubbed the "Twitter Revolution" by Western journalists—though not by Shirky himself, whose belief that Internet-enabled networking "can help loosely coordinated publics demand change" was a more nuanced expression of what too many today still accept as a self-evident truth, that the Internet can create instant revolution via inherently democratic open and decentralized leadership.[113] As Charlie Beckett wrote in 2011, the digital networks in Tunisia and Egypt during the Arab Spring were organized around "nodal figures who all tended to resist conventional leadership roles." Beckett in part ascribed what he called the "diffuse, horizontal nature" of the Arab Spring movements to the decentralized nature of the Internet itself, and he found this structure "very difficult [for governments] to break."[114]

"Dispersed but still connected," Philip Seib wrote in *Real-Time Diplomacy,* "that is the basic geography of [digital] networks. It was a perfect model for the agents of change during the Arab Spring."[115] Seib's view harks back to the early Electronic Frontier Foundation vision of cyberspace as a de facto state independent of any physical nation or leader.

The horrors of civil warfare in Syria and the brutal rise of ISIS, as well as the retrograde movement to military rule in Egypt, the strangely neglected chaos in Libya, and the reactionary religiosity of Tunisia have all made it increasing difficult to believe uncritically in the transcendent qualities of so-called cyberspace. And if, despite these grim realities, one still struggles to believe that the Internet's ability to transcend nations and borders is limitless, all that is necessary is to look at the likes of China. Intensively networked within its own borders, China's connections to the greater global Internet are nevertheless so severely curtailed, intensively filtered, and strictly controlled that some have called the barriers the modern equivalent of the Great Wall.

The fact is that, despite the ethereal, other-dimensional name we give it, "cyberspace" is the product of *physical* infrastructure that can be owned, operated, and controlled by governments. Internet data enters and leaves China at relatively few points, each of which is regulated by sophisticated gateway router systems built not by the Chinese themselves but by U.S.-based Cisco, a leading innovator in networking hardware. The bold and hopeful declarations of early Internet visionaries notwithstanding, the legal, coercive, and technological power of nation-states very significantly limits the capability of the Internet to transcend governments and create a genuinely global community, let alone a digital super state.

On April 11 2000, Mark Knobel, a French Jew acting on behalf of the International League against Racism, brought suit, in France, against Yahoo, which hosted an online auction website dealing in Nazi memorabilia. Knobel's suit alleged that Yahoo violated a French law banning trafficking Nazi artifacts and merchandise. While Knobel acknowledged that the auction might not be illegal in the United States, home of Yahoo, it was illegal once it had crossed into French territory.[116]

Yahoo responded to the suit by protesting that *French* law had no jurisdiction over Yahoo's *California*-based servers and that, furthermore, the company could not stop the free flow of data across cyberspace, a medium that effectively "eras[ed] boundaries." Knobel countered that international companies are routinely bound to abide by the laws of each of the countries in which they do business, regardless of their nation of domicile. Ford Motor Company, for instance, was obliged to obey the safety laws of France in order to sell its cars there. Yahoo countered that *cyberspace* companies were fundamentally different from companies that operated in *real space,* and offered an "impossibility defense," arguing that it was impossible for it to selectively prevent given websites from being seen in France.

As many at the time saw it, this defense was golden. Cyberspace, after all, respected no borders. (Everybody knew that!) It was energy and ether, not metal and plastic. But Knobel's legal team ultimately argued that new technologies existed that were in fact capable of identifying and screening Internet content on the basis of its geographical source. Indeed, the team pointed out that Yahoo's traffic into France came not directly from U.S.-based servers, but from servers located in Sweden. They argued that if U.S.-domiciled Yahoo "could target French users from Swedish servers, it could potentially identify users by geography and, if it liked, screen them out." This technology-based argument carried the day against Yahoo's technology-based impossibility defense, and, on November 20, 2000, Yahoo was instructed to make a reasonable "best effort" to block French users from access to the Nazi e-commerce website.[117]

The verdict of the French court may be seen as a watershed marking the beginning of the end of the Internet as an planetary force behind the regulation of terrestrial states. By the end of the first decade of the new century, many new technologies were making it routinely possible for "content delivery companies" to selectively craft and target ads and other data on the basis of geography or other criteria. It was no longer "impossible" to control the Internet in conformity with national laws, regulations, and even censorship requirements. These days, Yahoo and many other Internet-based companies create self-censored offerings for selected markets, such as the giant market that is China.

Technology has segmented cyberspace. Geo-political borders are now reflected in the Internet. Moreover, government control is enshrined in the very fabric of the Internet by the U.S. government's assertion of so-called "root authority"—the naming and numbering system on which operation of the "global" Internet depends.[118]

Even without such inherently coercive control, however, populations continually impose their preferences on the Internet. No owner/operator of a website interested in appealing, say, to French users, would attempt to impose upon France all English-language content strictly devoted to U.S. issues. Fail to appeal to the French with a language and content relevant to them, and your website will fail—in France. Increasingly, Internet technology is moving toward a greater and greater capability of targeting content to groups (defined by national, religious, regional, or interest-based criteria), some large, some very small and very specific. For e-commerce marketers, such customization even reaches the level of individual users. As part of this trend, cyberspace is evolving as less indiscriminately global and more sharply bordered.

The technology that enables e-commerce operators to identify groups and even individuals by needs, wants, desires, preferences, and buying habits can also enable governments—whether democratic or authoritarian—to identify, monitor, and ultimately threaten, arrest, or otherwise punish dissident groups and troublesome individuals. The anonymity of the Internet is fast eroding.

On a larger scale is the bordered nature of the physical infrastructure of so-called *cyberspace*. Appealing as that term is, "cyberspace" is largely a fiction. While "Ethernet" describes a family of networking technologies, there is nothing *ethereal* about the infrastructure to which the term is applied. Its constituents are copper, plastic, "fiber," silicon, and the like. Similarly, all of the phenomena of "cyberspace" first and last take place in physical space, over cables, through connectors, and via various material configurations of printed circuitry and semiconductors. While wireless satellite and tower-based transmission may be involved at some points, the "Internet backbone"—the principal data routes between large computer networks and core routers—is mainly physical and subject to gateways that are possessed and controlled by governments. A nation such as China, for instance, though intensively networked within its own borders, provides comparatively few cross-border gateways for the entrance and exit of global Internet infrastructure. The government treats these as carefully monitored choke points, and in this way maintains economically vital connections with the world, yet largely on terms that suit the official agenda.

Cyber realism

It is as unrealistic to ignore the impact of global digital interconnectivity on international commerce, politics, policy, and popular empowerment as it is to believe that the Internet has rendered traditional concepts of the nation state, sovereignty, nationalism, citizenship, loyalty, common interests, and common enmities obsolete. Cyberdiplomacy exists now and will become increasingly prevalent and important in time to come, but it cannot and will not simply displace and replace the most basic understanding and principles of international relations.

Where the future of international politics and policy is concerned, both cyber utopianism and approaches that acknowledge nothing other than analog realities are inadequate and destructive. Cyber realism, which takes into account the instrumentality and human effect of networked digital technology without forsaking the elements of diplomacy, law, and politics, is essential to the successful integration of the Internet into the global community.

CHAPTER 4
WIDE OPEN SECRECY

Evgeny Morozov[119] and other critics of the cyber-utopian vision of the Internet as an unalloyed "liberation technology" document how authoritarian states can manage to turn the Internet to decidedly anti-democratic purposes. Social media, for instance, which the cyber-utopianists cite as the instrument, vehicle, and (sometimes) the very agency of revolution, can be turned by oppressive regimes against activist users, betraying their identities, location, and connections. Facebook and similar peer-to-peer social platforms can be readily used as powerful means of surveillance. Moreover, despite a pervasive belief—especially among citizens of Western democracies—that the technology of the Internet enables it to transcend all political and even physical borders so that it cannot be bounded by the dictates of a particular regime or ideology, Morozov and Jack Goldsmith and Tim Wu[120] remind us that so-called cyberspace is not a creature of the all-pervading ether, but, in fact, travels along a hardware infrastructure of copper cable, fiber optics, and many routers and switches, most, if not all, of which are actually or potentially subject to government control. Given the right hardware and software—much of it supplied by US-based companies—an authoritarian regime can selectively block websites or website contents from crossing the borders it controls.

Such doses of cyber-realism are sobering antidotes to excessive cyber-utopianism, which, it is clear, consists at least in some degree of technologically uniformed magical thinking. Worse, many of the critics also turn an accusatory finger back upon the Western democracies—the United States paramount among them, pointing out many hypocritical instances of incursion upon Internet freedom.

The American Way

Evgeny Morozov writes that a truly free Internet—one "unburdened by regulation" of any kind—"is likely to be as conducive to democratization as a government unburdened by rule of law."[121] In other words, very far from "conducive." For this reason, he believes that "Western governments are poised to feel—and many of them are already feeling—growing pressure to regulate [the Internet]."[122] In the United States, this attitude often juxtaposes "American diplomats ... preaching the virtues of a free and open Internet abroad" against "their counterparts in domestic law enforcement, security, and military agencies ... preaching ... policies informed by a diametrically opposite assessment of those virtues."[123] James Lewis, senior fellow at the Center for Strategic and International Studies (Washington, DC), has characterized cyberspace as "increasingly Hobbesian," standing in blatant contradiction to the vision of early cyber-utopianists who believed "that a 'social contract' would emerge naturally from the self-organizing internet community without the intervention of the state."[124]

Support for this Hobbesian view has been provided by the pandemic of "fake news" churned out in particular by Russian sources and disseminated via social media and video hosting platforms that are for the most part entirely unregulated. Senator Al Franken (D-Minn) grilled a Facebook executive at a Senate hearing in October 2017 about how Facebook was helpless to discover Russian interference in the 2016 US general election when political ads were paid for with Russian rubles:

"People are buying ads on your platform with rubles," Franken said, his voice rising. "They're political ads. You put billions of data points together all the time — that's what I hear that these platforms do."

[Facebook General Counsel Colin] Stretch admitted that the company was policing advertisers for other abuses and that it failed to connect the dots on the two variables.

"Senator, it's a signal we should have been alert to, and in hindsight it's one we missed," Stretch said.

But despite repeated attempts by Franken, Stretch would not commit to saying Facebook would stop accepting foreign currencies for U.S. political ads.

"I can tell you that we're not going to permit political advertising by foreign actors," Stretch said. "The reason I'm hesitating on foreign currency is that it's relatively easy for bad actors to switch currency. It's a signal, but it's not enough — we have to sweep more broadly."[125]

The Internet, with social media sites unfettered by the kinds of U.S. government regulations that constrain radio and television, opens Americans to all points of view—including those expressly crafted to deceive and thereby (mis)guide electoral choice. No wonder that, in an effort to make the Internet a less Hobbesian environment, Western governments have been "flirting with censorship schemes that bear an eerie resemblance to those of China," according to Morozov.[126] But even when the government does not impose censorship, American users of the Internet, free as they are to browse, do not do what American policymakers claim as one of the greatest opportunities the technology affords. They do not explore other systems of government in an effort to find models for improving that of their own country. As recent US political campaigns have shown—especially that of Barack Obama in 2008—even if Americans don't window shop for better government, campaign managers are eager to make certain that they see displays of their candidate's wares. Yet, in world of e-commerce that has developed a high degree of sophistication in targeting individual Internet users based on their interests as demonstrated by (among other things) their Internet browsing habits, political campaigns persist in simply spamming everyone. Before the Internet age, a campaign staff had to work hard to get the word out, and so, of necessity, tended to carefully target likely supporters. Today, the click of a mouse will blast hundreds or thousands or tens of thousands of emails more or less indiscriminately. The marginal cost of this spamming, whether measured in effort or cash, is vanishingly small. The cost in voter motivation and passion frittered away by message fatigue is, however, impossible to calculate—and, apparently, nobody ever tries.

Lessons from eCommerce

But what if politicians and government bureaucrats eschewed brute-force spamming and began to adopt the high technology of today's e-commerce advertisers? We think of ourselves in a wide variety of ways: as fathers, mothers, sons, daughters, teachers, lawyers, doctors, football heroes, racecar drivers, citizens, taxpayers, voters, shoppers, whatever. We do not typically think of ourselves as what the European Union's European Commission called us in 2012: *data subjects*. Yet this is precisely how advertisers think of us. That is how they first encounter us, get to know us, track us, and study each one of us. Not as a person, let alone a "private person," but as a *data subject*.[127]

This treatment has been going on for some time. A 2010 *Wall Street Journal* article reported that the top fifty US websites were each installing an average of sixty-four pieces of tracking technology, usually without notice, on each computer that visited their sites.[128] These software programs are the instruments of online behavioral targeting, better known in the Internet advertising and marketing industry as *online behavioral advertising*—OBA, for short. The tracking software works like this: You visit a web site, and the OBA software tracks the pages you visit, the amount of time you view each page, the links you click on, the searches you make, and the items you interact with. The software allows the website to collect this data, which may be collated with other factors to create a "profile" linked to your web browser. The owner or publisher of the website can use such data, tracked from thousands of visitors, to define audience "segments," each segment composed of visitors with similar profiles. When you return to a specific site or a specific network of sites (provided you use the same web browser to do so), advertisers can use your profile information to position their online ads in front of you (and other visitors with similar profiles) on the assumption that you will likely be interested in the advertiser's particular merchandise or service. Instead of randomly placing ads, the advertiser is able to target you based on the interests your profile reveals. OBA becomes increasingly accurate over time, as your profile accretes more data and becomes more complete. Companies called "advertising networks" or "ad nets" deliver ads to, and track users across, not a single website but networks of sites. This enables them to assemble rather detailed pictures of the demographic makeup of a large swath of Internet users. In this way, an ad network can sell advertisers exposure to specific audiences rather than merely a spot on specific websites.

Not long ago, OBA was the cutting edge of targeted online advertising. According to a 2009 study, OBA could increase click-through rates by as much as 670 percent. The click-through rate—what insiders call CTR—is a common yardstick for measuring the success of an online advertising campaign at a particular website. CTR is defined as the number of clicks on an ad divided by the number of times the ad is shown (this number is referred to as "impressions"). The quotient is expressed as a percentage. That is, if an ad is shown 100 times (delivers 100 "impressions") and users are sufficiently intrigued to click on it 25 times, the CTR of that particular ad is 0.25, or 25 percent.[129]

While it is still a workhorse of e-commerce, OBA no longer represents the state of the art in consumer tracking. Newer technologies reach out from behind the behind the monitor screen and into the "real world." On July 14, 2013, for example, the high-end retailer Nordstrom told the *New York Times* that it had experimented with tracking customer's movements using Wi-Fi signals from their smartphones.

While the signals are invisible, Nordstrom put up a sign telling customers they were being tracked. Customers complained, and Nordstrom ended the experiment.[130]

While consumers have become accustomed to being tracked online, many are made uneasy when the practice is extended into physical space. It would not be so bad if retailers were only trying to map customer movement through the store, but they may also grab metadata—the phone's MAC (media access control) address, a unique identifier that opens up a world of cross-reference data. With the MAC address, all sorts of public and commercial information about the customer can be accessed to build a profile, including, for instance, income, Zip code, and other online and offline nuggets. A middle-aged middle school principal may—*may*—resent being through the lingerie department, but *he* will be even more uncomfortable to discover that his retail foray is being collated with his record of online browsing, his Facebook, Twitter, and LinkedIn presence on the social web, and so on. The walls that formerly separated physical space from cyberspace are dissolving.

In-store devices that measure signal strength between a smartphone's WiFi card and a WiFi hotspot (transmitter) can pinpoint a shopper's location. Other systems use inexpensive RFID (radio-frequency identification) tags attached to merchandise to communicate with the smartphone's Bluetooth radio, telling the retailer when a customer is close to a particular item or display. Still other systems communicate with the MEMS (microelectromechanical systems) in many smartphones, including the accelerometer chip that knows when the phone is being held right side up or sideways and the magnetometer that serves as a compass. With this information, it is possible to track customer movement even more accurately.

Any even mildly determined government can readily adapt the data capture and analytical technology and practices already widely used by marketers to track online browsing as well as shoppers moving through physical space. How much of this will citizens be willing to tolerate? And about how much of it will they even be aware?

A private-public partnership

There is evidence of the private sector's willingness not merely to tolerate but actually to facilitate government incursions into privacy, even in the democratic United States. In keeping with its much-publicized (and often mocked) corporate mantra, "Don't be evil," Google is a key member of the Global Network Initiative (GNI). According to its website, GNI was founded in response to the "increasing ... pressure" from governments "all over the world—from the Americas to Europe to the Middle East to Africa and Asia" exerted upon "companies in the Information & Communications Technology (ICT) sector ... to comply with domestic laws and policies in ways that may conflict with the internationally recognized human rights of freedom of expression and privacy." GNI was the product of two years of work among "a multi-stakeholder group of companies [Google prominent among them], civil society organizations (including human rights and press freedom groups), investors and academics" to create "a collaborative approach to protect and advance freedom of expression and privacy in the ICT sector."[131]

Despite its GNI membership, Google has been criticized for an "increasingly carefree attitude toward privacy,"[132] and in the summer of 2013, it was revealed that Google, Yahoo, and other tech companies were paid by the United States, via the National Security Agency (NSA), to comply with the agency's massive PRISM surveillance program.[133] Launched by NSA in 2007, in coordination and cooperation with GCHQ (NSA's UK counterpart), PRISM is (as of 2015) a still-active clandestine mass electronic surveillance data-mining program. Under authority defined by Section 207 of the FISA Amendment Act of 2008, PRISM collects Internet communications (data) from Internet companies (Google et al) and is "the number one source of raw intelligence used for NSA analytic reports," accounting for 91 percent of the Internet traffic NSA acquires under Section 702 authority."[134] Yahoo, we now know, was not so willing to comply and brought a secret—and unsuccessful—lawsuit to resist the NSA's demands for PRISM compliance, demands backed by threats of ruinous fines: "$250,000 daily ... set to double 'every week.'"[135]

But others in private sector have encouraged a far more trusting attitude. In a 2013 *USA Today* article rather blithely headlined "Latest PRISM disclosures shouldn't worry consumers," Tom Kellermann, vice president of cybersecurity for global security software maker Trend Micro, was quoted: "The people who work on PRISM are working to protect us. They don't care what movie you're going to or whether someone is cheating on his wife." General Keith Alexander, director of the NSA, reported in 2013 that PRISM had helped the FBI stop 54 terrorist attacks in the US and other nations, and Chris Petersen, chief technology officer at security analytics company LogRhythm, has remarked that PRISM "really has no bearing on the average citizen." His explanation for this judgment is rather less soothing, however. "The big revelation is that the NSA is actually able to view more encrypted data than anyone thought. What this will really do is put our adversaries on notice that they need to invest in stronger encryption."[136] So Petersen seems to be saying that the only people and organizations NSA deliberately targets are those who encrypt data—those with secrets to hide, a category that presumably excludes the "average citizen." For him, the downside is not the program's threat to privacy, but the incentive it offers "our adversaries" out in the world to up their game by investing in stronger encryption.

The Snowden and Manning leaks

That Chris Petersen used the phrase "big revelation" is, of course, highly significant. For the United States government most certainly did not suddenly disclose information about PRISM in a voluntary fit of transparency.

Edward Snowden was a Booz Allen Hamilton consultant doing contract work for the NSA at an agency facility in Hawaii. He had been a system administrator for the Central Intelligence Agency (CIA) and a counterintelligence trainer for the Defense Intelligence Agency (DIA). Dell Computer later hired him to do contract work at NSA facilities in the United States and Japan. He left Dell in March 2013 to work for Booz Allen Hamilton. A seasoned IT professional, Snowden had no known history of political activism or whistleblowing when, in June 2013, he was thrust onto the global stage after leaking thousands of classified NSA documents collected while he worked for Dell and Booz Allen. The documents exposed global surveillance programs—including PRISM—run by the NSA and by the so-called Five Eyes, an alliance consisting of intelligence agencies in Australia, Canada, New Zealand, the UK, and the United States.

Before actually leaking the documents he held, Snowden left Hawaii on May 13, 2013, for Hong Kong, in the People's Republic of China. Here, in June, he began releasing documents, showing many to journalists Glenn Greenwald and Laura Poitras, whom he had summoned to a meeting in Hong Kong. On June 9, Snowden publicly revealed himself, and on June 14 the US federal government charged him with violation of the Espionage Act and theft of government property. Now a fugitive, Snowden left Hong Kong on June 23 and flew to Moscow, where he was accommodated in the "transit zone" of Sheremetyevo International Airport for thirty-nine days while he applied for political asylum in 21 countries. Granted "temporary" asylum in Russia on August 1, 2013, he has been living in that country—his precise location undisclosed—ever since. His subsequent applications for asylum in the EU have all, as of 2015, been rejected.

Both within the United States and globally, Snowden has drawn both praise (as a heroic whistleblower) and condemnation (as a self-righteous traitor who has endangered Western security). The first of Snowden's documents were published simultaneously by *The Washington Post* and *The Guardian*, with releases continuing throughout 2013. Subsequently, *The New York Times*, the Canadian Broadcasting Corporation, the Australian Broadcasting Corporation, *Der Spiegel* (in Germany), *O Globo* (Brazil), *Le Monde* (France), *L'espresso* (Italy), *NRC Handelsblad* (the Netherlands), *Dagbladet* (Norway), *El País* (Spain), and *Sveriges Television* (Sweden) published additional leaked documents. Although the total published leak has been voluminous, as of 2015 it represents only a small fraction of an estimated trove of 1.7 million documents.

While revelations about the NSA PRISM program and a program analyzing huge volumes of telephone metadata have captured most of the attention of the press and public, perhaps of even greater consequence are revelations of secret treaties (including one dating to 1954) signed by Western powers for the purpose of implementing surveillance on a global scale. Under these secret covenants, Germany and Sweden share data with the NSA, and the NSA sends to Israel raw and unfiltered data collected from its surveillance of US citizens. The intelligence services of other nations, including Australia, Canada, Denmark, France, Italy, the Netherlands, Norway, Spain, Switzerland, and the UK, cooperatively participate with the United States in global digital surveillance activities.

The Snowden documents were published against the backdrop of an earlier set of revelations in the form of documents, photographs, and videos leaked by US Army private Bradley Edward Manning (a transgender person who now identifies herself as a woman, Chelsea Elizabeth Manning).

Manning grew up in a dysfunctional family, was tormented by personal emotional conflict arising from gender identity disorder, lived as a gay man, and subsisted on a series of low-paying jobs. In 2007, Manning's father (who had been an intelligence analyst in the US Navy) persuaded him (prior to August 22, 2013, Manning publicly identified himself as a man[137]) to enlist in the US Army. Seeing the possibility of a college education on the G. I. Bill and apparently hoping that the masculine military environment would help to resolve his gender identity disorder, Manning enlisted in September 2007. Small, slight, effeminate, and isolated, Manning was bullied but fought back. While still in basic training, he was transferred to a discharge unit, destined for separation from the Army. The discharge decision was revoked, however, and after completing basic training, Manning was given advanced trained as an intelligence analyst. He then received a Top Secret/Sensitive Compartmented Information security clearance.

Despite obvious adjustment and emotional problems, Manning was additionally trained for forward deployment to Iraq, where intelligence analysts were in critically short supply. Deployed to a base near Baghdad, Manning had access to networks carrying sensitive and top secret information, performing his duties adequately enough to receive the Global War on Terrorism Service Medal and a promotion from Private First Class to Specialist. At this time, he made known a desire for sex reassignment surgery, became increasingly opposed to the war in Iraq, and complained of feeling intensely isolated and lonely. Manning sent an email to his supervisor advising him of his gender identity disorder (he attached a jpeg showing him dressed as a woman) and then began a demonstrative downward emotional spiral, during which he was demoted back to PFC, assigned to work in a supply office, but never stripped of his lofty security clearances.

In a message to threat analyst and self-confessed convicted hacker Adrian Lamo, Manning later described his situation this way: "deployed to eastern baghdad, pending discharge for 'adjustment disorder' in lieu of 'gender identity disorder.'" If we take this at face value, it means that the US Army put a soldier of the lowest post-basic rank in a highly sensitive position even though (as Manning told Lamo) he was in trouble for "revealing my uncertainty over my gender identity . . . which is causing me to lose this job" although "i managed to keep my security clearance so far." This gave him "free reign [sic] over classified networks for long periods of time." The documents he saw were "incredible things, awful things ... things that belonged in the public domain, and not on some server stored in a dark room in Washington DC"—yet fully accessible to him in an outpost in Iraq, and ridiculously easy to obtain: "weak servers, weak logging, weak physical security, weak counter-intelligence, inattentive signal analysis ... a perfect storm."[138]

Manning would later be charged with (among other crimes) stealing secret documents. Assessing the situation objectively, it is clear that the army more or less left its secrets out for the taking. In a message sent at 1:13:10 p.m. on May 21, 2010, Manning presented himself to Lamo as a moral martyr: "i wouldn't mind going to prison for the rest of my life, or being executed," only to worry about "the possibility of having pictures of me ... plastered all over the world press ... as [a] boy ...." A minute later, at 1:14:11 p.m., he called himself just crazy: "I've totally lost my mind ... i make no sense ... the CPU is not made for this motherboard ..."[139]

Manning told Lamo that he had developed a working relationship with Julian Assange, cofounder and editor-in-chief of the website WikiLeaks, with whom he regularly communicated via an encrypted Internet conferencing service. He began leaking sensitive and secret material to Assange, including diplomatic cables and Department of Defense documents, among them a video that became known as the "Collateral Murder" video. It showed a pair of US helicopters firing on a group of ten men in Baghdad--two of them Reuters employees photographing a US Army Humvee under attack. The American helicopter pilots mistook the journalists' cameras for weapons and fired not only on them, but on a van that had stopped to help men wounded in an earlier inadvertent attack by US helicopters. Two children in the van were wounded and their father was killed.[140] Assange released the video on April 5, 2010, and WikiLeaks was suddenly catapulted to public attention.

All told, the Manning material released by WikiLeaks between April and November 2010 would ultimately amount to 251,287 US diplomatic cables, more than 400,000 classified US Army reports from the Iraq War, and some 90,000 on Afghanistan, plus disturbing videos. Yet whatever Manning was or is, he was not and is not a master hacker or spy. The "massive data spillage," he told Lamo, was "facilitated by numerous factors . . . both physically, technically, and culturally." It was a "perfect example of how not to do INFOSEC [information security]." He concluded by declaring that "information should be free,"[141] a paraphrase of the famous line "Information wants to be free," attributed to *Whole Earth Catalog* founder Stewart brand and first uttered (perhaps) at the Hacker's Conference of 1984.

Can there be diplomacy without secrets?

Before returning to the Snowden leaks, let us pause to earnestly ask: *Does information* really *want to be free—including the information of diplomacy?*

The very first of President Woodrow Wilson's famous "Fourteen Points" of 1918—what he called "our program . . . of the world's peace"—was the abolition of "private international understandings of any kind" in favor of "diplomacy [that] shall proceed always frankly and in the public view."[142] Secret agreements, Wilson believed, had plunged the world into world war. A year earlier, however, Wilson had signed into law the Espionage Act of 1917, under which the likes of Julius and Ethel Rosenberg, Daniel Ellsberg, Bradley Manning, and Edward Snowden would be charged in connection with revealing state secrets.

On August 20, 2012, filmmakers Michael Moore and Oliver Stone published an op ed in *The New York Times* applauding Ecuador for protecting Julian Assange against extradition to Sweden for questioning about a sexual assault. Moore and Stone argued that the extradition was a prelude to extradition to the United States, presumably to face charges relating to the Manning leaks.[143]

For Moore and Stone, the issues were human rights and freedom of speech. I would suggest, however, that the issues in the Manning (and Snowden) cases are not so clear cut. The cognitive dissonance President Wilson exhibited concerning secrecy—renouncing it even as he enshrined it in law—is certainly endemic to our nation and perhaps to nationhood generally. Julian Assange did not hack into a top secret computer. He published what Bradley Manning gave him. Manning is charged (among other things) with "theft of public property or records," yet—and here is where the cognitive dissonance really begins to kick in—it is hard to call how Manning obtained the unprecedented trove of documents "stealing" or even "hacking."

Did the US Army *want* that information to be free? Did Woodrow Wilson, signer of the Espionage Act of 1917, *want* diplomacy without secrets?

I don't believe these questions can be definitively answered, but if we at least ask them, we must come to the conclusion that cognitive dissonance is viable neither as a security policy nor a diplomatic policy. If there is a lesson in the "perfect storm" of Assange, Manning, and Manning's obtuse, uncaring, and negligent US Army commanders and supervisors, it is to find ways to set *openness* as a baseline for diplomacy, with deviations into *secrecy* made selectively and only upon careful thought. With fewer secrets to defend, defending them becomes a feasible management task, provided that a high value is put on this core of data, the keys to which must be closely held rather than made accessible on a server in a remote Middle Eastern outpost manned by a lonely and tormented private on the verge of discharge.

As for Julian Assange, the narrative of WikiLeaks as a selfless experiment in ending dangerous diplomatic secrecy by outing everything freely across the Internet was shattered by WikiLeak's role in disrupting the 2016 United States general election. In light of a growing mountain of evidence, all but the most naïve among us can escape the conclusion that, for whatever reasons, Assange and his online enterprise have become tools of Russian intelligence. Indeed, WikiLeaks appears to have served as a Russian front in 2016.[144] WikiLeaks indeed appears to have begun as a kind of equal-opportunity outer of secrets: "In the first three years of its existence," Jonathan Foreman wrote in *Commentary* back in 2011, "WikiLeaks received and published hitherto secret documents concerning a wide variety of entities around the world," but began in 2010 to turn its focus on the U.S. government.[145] In 2017, the conservative historian Max Boot put it this way in a *Foreign Policy* headline: "WikiLeaks Has Joined the Trump Administration."[146]

The Casablanca *Solution*

"Three may keep a secret, if two of them are dead," Ben Franklin's Poor Richard observed back in the mid-eighteenth century. Flash forward to November 1, 2012, when the Office of the Director of National Intelligence revealed that 4,917,751 people were privy to confidential, secret, or top secret documents. (Washington, D.C. population at the time = 632,323.) Of these nearly five million secret sharers, 1,409,969 held the very highest (top secret) clearance. Among these were 135,506 private contractors, a category that included Edward Snowden.[147]

Snowden has been labeled contractor, whistleblower, "transparency advocate,"[148] hero, spy, and traitor.[149] Here's another label: *diplomatic provocateur.* Not only did Snowden provide China and Russia with an opportunity to invert an old-school Cold War scenario by sheltering a "dissident," his revelations have exacerbated US-EU discord over issues of digital privacy. The dispute went public on January 25, 2012, when the European Commission released a proposed regulation limiting data collection and Internet user tracking by e-commerce providers, including American firms doing business in the EU.[150] Snowden's revelations now extend the dispute from objections to the data-gathering practices of US-based companies to the practices of the US government.

The weekly International Association of Privacy Professionals (IAPP) publication *Data Protection Digest* headlined its June 2, 2013 lead story "Will NSA Revelations Be a Game Changer?"[151] Leaders of US-based firms continue to speculate that the NSA leaks will prompt the EU to another data protection rewrite, even more draconian than that of the January 2012 regulation, which US e-commerce providers vigorously protested. For their part, EU authorities (and others, of course) have expressed concern over reports of "increasingly deep connections between Silicon Valley and the [NSA]."[152] Viviane Reding, EU vice president and commissioner for justice, fundamental rights, and citizenship, expressed frustration after a joint press conference with US Attorney General Eric Holder in Dublin.[153] She is just one of "several EU officials" who, in the wake of the NSA leaks, "have called for more trust and transparency between the EU and US"—the "US" implicitly including the private sector, with its increasingly deep connections to the government and its intelligence apparatus.[154]

Trust requires transparency. But, by definition, secrecy is not transparent. It has long been a principle of international relations that nations must be able to maintain certain "state secrets" for the sake of their sovereignty and security. But a system in which "secrets" are shared by some *five million people* is neither transparent nor truly secret. It creates the liability of opacity—which destroys trust—without realizing the benefits of truly strategic secrecy. This has long been a dysfunctional intelligence strategy, but Snowden's leaks have given the EU's demands for transparency new urgency.

Snowden has declared the intention to expose the US as a "surveillance state."[155] It is now so exposed. Nevertheless, just what this provocative phrase means remains unclear. Snowden claims that he, an NSA contractor, could "at any time ... wiretap anyone—from you or your accountant, to a federal judge, to even the President." In Senate testimony, NSA director General Keith Alexander called the claim "false."[156] Does this terse denial constitute sufficient transparency? Of course not. Should the "surveillance state" be shut down? We cannot answer because we still do not know what that phrase means as applied to what is actually happening at NSA and other agencies. But if the question is simply *Should government surveillance be stopped?....* the simple answer is no. A nation's security has always depended on some amount of surveillance. And, in an era of global interconnectivity, the dependence is greater than ever.

At least 5 million people can claim to be as "shocked" by Snowden's revelations as *Casablanca*'s Captain Louis Renault was "shocked ... *shocked*" by the "revelation" of gambling in Rick's Café Américain. The rest of us? Well, we weren't really surprised, either. CIA and NSA surveillance are products of a surveillance program far less secret than opaque. The opacity, more than the secrecy, has provoked an international crisis of trust. It implies an obvious course of resolution: replace opacity with transparency.

It could begin this way: The US president sends an agent to reconnoiter any liquor store in Washington, DC. The operative reports finding a sign prominently displayed: *These Premises Are Under Surveillance.* The president responds by ordering the national security apparatus to immediately adopt the liquor store model.

Everyone everywhere already feels they are being watched and listened to. Why not tell them—officially—that they are quite right? We *are*, all of us, under surveillance. Just be sure to define "surveillance" transparently. Such a definition is certain to fall far short of a policy of random and omniscient eavesdropping that the public, in the absence of transparency, imagines.

Two of the biggest online players, Microsoft and—yes—Google have taken the lead on transparency by seeking permission to publish statistics on the number of data requests they receive from the government.[157] Clearly, the companies believe that revealing the actually small number of requests will show that they are not cavalierly betraying their customers by dumping user data in the lap of the NSA, FBI, or CIA. Publishing the volume of requests will create transparency without compromising actual secrets.

Having rationally defined "surveillance," the administration's next step should be earning the buy-in of the American people by making a clear case for the necessity of the current surveillance programs. Succeed in persuading the American people that rationally limited surveillance furthers the constitutional mandate to "provide for the common defense" and buy-in becomes an attainable goal.

To earn commensurate buy-in from global allies and trading partners, begin by paring down state secrets to a bare minimum accessible to a very few (i.e., > 5 million). Next, transparently explain how this modest cache of secrets serves the security of the United States *and* its allies. As for the rest, shed a bright light on it all. Celebrate wide-open secrecy.

Transparency will go a long way toward building trust and cooperation, but transparency alone is not enough. On May 14, 2008, NATO took the forward-looking step of creating the Cooperative Cyber Defense Centre of Excellence (CCDCOE) in Tallinn, Estonia. CCDCOE's stated mission is

"to enhance the capability, cooperation and information sharing among NATO, NATO nations and partners in cyber defence by virtue of education, research and development, lessons learned and consultation." Its "vision is to be the main source of expertise in the field of cooperative cyber defence by accumulating, creating, and disseminating knowledge in related matters within NATO, NATO nations and partners."[158]

Since the dissolution of the Soviet Union in 1991, many NATO members have questioned the continued need for the alliance. Cybersecurity, including surveillance in cyberspace, is precisely that need. It makes sense, therefore, to use the CCDCOE to give all NATO members a voice and a stake in issues of cybersecurity, surveillance, and privacy. This will not only foster the trust, confidence, and cooperation of a formal alliance, but, further, will help all member nations, including the United States, make their cyber-related programs both more effective and more secure.

NATO deterred aggression throughout the Cold War. NATO can now be leveraged to do in cyberspace what it did in geopolitical space. Moreover, a set of cyber policies shared among twenty-eight member nations rather than imposed by a single nation, the United States, is more likely to gain broad global acceptance. "Surveillance state"? Whatever else the Snowden leaks did and may yet do, they reveal the existence of far more than a surveillance *state*. The Internet creates a surveillance *planet*, and we have an opportunity and responsibility to work toward global policies to help us live securely, freely, and productively upon it.

The NSA and Big Data: crazy stupid love

In 2010, Google's Eric Schmidt told attendees at the Techonomy conference in Lake Tahoe that humanity was now creating as much information every two days as it created between the dawn of civilization and 2003: every 48 hours, 5 exabytes, or 5 quintillion bytes (5 followed by 18 zeros).[159]

A stunning statistic? Even more stunning is the apparent fact that the NSA intends to capture pretty much every one of those bytes every second of every day—forever. In a world in which several terabytes (1 TB = 1,000,000,000,000 bytes) can fit on what is nowadays an inexpensive solid state drive (SSD) the size of a credit card, how else to explain the perceived need for the massive $1.5 billion NSA facility completed in May 2014 in the shadow of Utah's Wasatch Range—an edifice "more than five times the size of the US Capitol"?[160]

No wonder the agency faced in 2013 (and continues to face it) what Hoover Institution fellows Amy Zegart and Marshall Erwin have called "the worst crisis in its 60-year history."[161] Utah's massive monument to surveillance speaks far louder and much more clearly than anything NSA leaders have said to explain and justify the agency's mission. Does the NSA exist to discover terrorist "chatter" and outright plots? Does it function to keep Americans safe, and to prevent the next 9/11? From all appearances, given a building 6.5 million cubic feet large, the scope of the NSA mission is to track everything and spy on everyone all of the time.

Facing its worst crisis of image ever, the NSA needs to rebrand itself and, in so doing, rebrand the United States government's stance toward the Internet in which it has a special moral and owner stake. In defending the image of the agency against the leaks of Edward Snowden, NSA director General Keith Alexander (2005-2014) accused the media of exaggerating the scope of NSA surveillance programs and suggested that if Americans only understood what the agency actually does, their anxieties over Big Brother would be allayed and their appreciation for the mission greatly increased.[162] So, if what General Alexander said is correct—that the more we know about the NSA, the more we will support what it does—then the obvious first step toward rebranding is a combination of transparency and education. Come clean about the mission—not the nitty-gritty details, perhaps, but the scope and purpose—and explain NSA in a way that corrects both the alleged media hype and the impression created by that really, really big building in Utah.

An October 2013 poll commissioned by the Hoover Institution in effect tested Alexander's assertion. As Zegart and Erwin explained, "Our initial hunch was that Americans knew little about the intelligence agencies that have kept us safe since 9/11, and that public ignorance was compounding the NSA's trust problems." What the poll demonstrated, however, is that ignorance not only did *not* breed greater distrust of the NSA, but "the more that Americans understand the NSA's activities, the less they support the agency." For example: "Among those who erroneously believed the NSA conducts operations to kill terrorists, 35% had an unfavorable view of the agency. Among those who answered this question correctly, 64% viewed the NSA unfavorably."[163]

It turns out that rehabilitating the NSA brand takes more than transparency and education. It takes compelling proof that NSA programs really are effective counter-terrorism tools. Obviously, providing this proof requires programs that are, in fact, effective. An absolute precondition for developing such programs is fringing to an end the agency's all-consuming love affair with Big Data. If Big Data is a haystack, the information we actually want—the useful information—is a needle. To find the terrorist threat—our coveted needle of useful information—why would we begin the search by making the Big Data haystack bigger?

The NSA mission is intelligence. All the data humanity produces every day is not intelligence. It is data—a lot of data. Intelligence is, well, intelligent. And the intelligent approach to collecting data is to identify the right data to collect, collect it, analyze it, and leave the rest of it alone.

If the NSA is to reclaim the value of its brand—and, with it, the diplomatic brand of the United States as moral leader—it needs to become an intelligent consumer of data rather than a compulsive hoarder, whose monstrously omnivorous habits elicit from the public sentiments including disgust, fear, outrage, and morbid curiosity. These are the emotional drivers of reality TV, not what the National Security Agency and the government it serves desperately need right now—which, by the way, are acceptance, support, and gratitude.

On the persistence of "meatspace"

On December 9, 2014, the 525 unclassified pages of a 6,000-page report on the CIA's post-9/11 "Detention and Interrogation Program" were released by the Senate Select Committee on Intelligence. The media immediately and all too aptly dubbed it "the torture report," and its release elicited dire predictions that publication would set into motion a wave of retaliatory terrorism, perhaps organized via social media and coordinated by mobile technology.

It is well known that both ISIS and al Qaeda make extensive use of the Internet. And recent history has shown that, with or without social media, religious extremists require very little prompting to commit terrorist acts. Terrorism, after all, is what terrorists do. Yet recent history also suggests that provocative documents do not invariably provoke terrorist attacks. The many ominous predictions that WikiLeaks' release of Chelsea Manning's purloined cache of military and diplomatic documents and Edward Snowden's NSA material would incite terrorism have not come true. (On the other hand, the leaking during 2016-2017 of NSA "hacking tools" exfiltrated from the NSA's own servers, has stirred great anxiety in the United States and elsewhere—as it should.[164])

The fears stirred by the airing of the CIA's obscenely dirty laundry via the Manning and Snowden leaks may be products of genuine concern or may be nothing more substantial than the artifacts of partisan resistance to criticism of Bush administration policy. That "the Democrat report" (as Republicans dubbed it) was condemned by every GOP legislator, save former POW and torture victim Senator John McCain, strongly suggests the latter. And those who were inclined to applaud the "torture report" as welcome evidence that the dull do-nothing 114th Congress was actually capable of meaningful action after all were unsurprisingly disappointed by a reception defined and divided, as always, strictly by party affiliation. A product of political action, the torture report appeared destined to do nothing more than further harden the prevailing Washington gridlock.

Nevertheless, the Senate Select Committee report, like the Manning documents and the Snowden leaks before it, has launched some *public,* if not legislative, conversations about whether secrecy, deception, and torture can ever be tolerated in a free society—even when the justification offered is as payment for the "cost of freedom," which, CIA apologists relentlessly remind us, "isn't free." Maybe, just maybe, the *public* conversation will shape itself into an instance of genuine and potent *populism* opposed to secrecy, deception, and torture in a government of, by, and for the people.

There are precedents. As we saw in Chapter 2, Internet activists are quick to point to recent popular political movements across the world— in the Philippines, Ukraine, and the Middle East—as evidence of the possibility of potent populism and public diplomacy. Perhaps the public conversation begun by the torture report will swell into a movement capable of breaking through the gridlock of Washington itself.

Perhaps. But the same recent history that suggests publication of the report will not produce terrorism also argues against the prospects for any public conversation, even amplified and ramified through the Web, evolving into a popular political movement capable of overcoming official legislative politics as usual. In any case, right now, the partisan monologue appears likely to shout down the public discourse. And—right now—the prospects appear dim for developing, let alone sustaining, an effective popular movement in *cyberspace*, whether in the form of domestic cyber politics or international cyberdiplomacy, to counter the enormities of policy, politics, and "diplomacy" reduced to torture. For Internet visionaries of an emerging cyber-politics and cyberdiplomacy, perhaps the cruelest revelation of the torture report is that the corrupt brutality of the real world—the realm they sometimes mock as "meatspace" in contrast to "cyberspace"—is extraordinarily durable in its sickening persistence.

Privacy is *security*

Speaking of things that are sickening in their persistence, key to making the transition from traditional analog diplomacy to a diplomacy that incorporates the digital realities of our civilization—a *cyberdiplomacy*—is shedding the rigorous yet arbitrary division of *security* and *privacy* into mutually exclusive categories. We are told that if we want to know something about *digital security*, we should consult sources on digital security. If we want to know something about *digital privacy,* we should turn to material devoted to digital privacy.

Most readers of the preceding admittedly tedious paragraph will detect a tautology. What I intended to convey, however, is an accurate representation of the state of affairs in our digital world, a state that is as bizarre as it is dysfunctional. As if in response to a blow from the doctor's rubber mallet, we automatically, without thought, kick "security" into the basket marked *security* and "privacy" into the other labeled *privacy.* And yet this reflexive separation of security and privacy hardly reflects the reality of the way we all live today, so thoroughly mediated by digital networks. It is the inevitable tendency of networked systems to connect rather than to divide. Digital reality therefore offers no neat and separate "baskets"—which means, among many other things, that "security" and "privacy" are neither separate nor separable but occupy one continuum along which sharp demarcation is not only counterproductive but actually impossible.

Nevertheless, we persist in trying to separate them.

This habit is dysfunctional enough when the "security" issues under discussion concern individual users and networks, and the topic is viruses, Trojans, phishing, and the like, and when "privacy" issues involve nothing more than the creepiness of cookie-based tracking, online behavioral advertising (OBA), and ads and offers pushed to a smartphone, triggered by geolocation technology. The false separation becomes urgently critical, however, when "security" is defined in collective rather than individual terms and "privacy" is seen as an issue of profound constitutional and human rights.

The Snowden leaks launched a debate pitting the NSA's claims that its mass collection and analysis of digital metadata protect national *security* against claims by privacy groups, rights organizations, and foreign governments (as well as some parts of the *United States* government) that such surveillance is an assault on *privacy* defined as a constitutional and human right. In short, most of us have escalated the separation of "security" and "privacy" from a dysfunctional habit of taxonomical convenience to an absolute moral and political dichotomy, as if the requirements of security preclude those of privacy and vice versa.

While it is both foolish and futile to deny that the digital networking of the planet has wrought profoundly transformative disruption—and has done so very rapidly—it is also a mistake to claim a hard separation between years BCE (*Before the Computer Era*) and CE (*Computer Era*). For the relationship between *security* and *privacy* was contemplated long before the dawn of the digital age. The United States Constitution is remarkably brief and non-specific—an outline that has been colored in and elaborated upon by more than two centuries of legislation and legal interpretation. The document nowhere mentions "privacy," for example, and yet decade upon decade of legislation and case law protect privacy based on the assertion of a constitutional guarantee.

Typically, the source of a "right" to privacy is identified as the Fourth Amendment: "The right of the people to be secure in their persons, houses, papers, and effects, against unreasonable searches and seizures, shall not be violated ..." Despite the absence of the word, *privacy* is clearly at issue here—especially with reference to "papers" and, perhaps somewhat less strongly, "effects." Significantly, the word that *is* prominent in the amendment is "secure." Thus, far from opposing *security* and *privacy,* the Constitution joins them by defining privacy in the very terms of security. What is *privacy*? It is being *secure* in your papers and effects.

I propose that, in our unfolding twenty-first century, we heed this synthesis made back in the eighteenth. In drafting the Fourth Amendment, James Madison did not merely posit a relationship between security and privacy but clearly understood that there can be no security without privacy and no privacy without security. It is time for us to recognize and honor this insight enshrined in a document ratified well over two hundred years ago. In doing so, we should also acknowledge the advantage—unknown and unknowable, of course, to Madison and his colleagues—that technology now confers upon us. Unlike the framers of the Constitution, we actually have no pressing need for such terms as *security* and *privacy,* at least not in a digital context. Once committed to keyboard and conveyed to the Web, both "security" and "privacy" become *data,* and thus issues of security or privacy become issues of *data control.*

Data control. It is a phrase wonderfully liberating in its cold neutrality, which contrasts so usefully with the heated subjectivity of *security* and *privacy,* qualities in large part defined by feelings. In a digital context, data control creates both security and privacy and, what is more, does not mistakenly distinguish between the two. In contrast to the emotionally charged subjectivity of those words, data control is a matter of objective, measurable fact—not an issue of competing rights and imperatives, but simply a matter of who's got access to your 0s and 1s.

So here is my modest proposal. Let's not only stop separating *security* from *privacy,* let alone opposing the one to the other. Let's forget *security* and forget *privacy* altogether and resolve instead to get control of our data.

New laws? Yes, we'll need them, and they will have to be global in scope. And there also remain legitimately contentious issues of who actually controls data going into a transaction online, during a transaction, and following it. For example, when you approach an online merchant you do so as a person, but by virtue of the transaction, you also become a customer. Does this give the merchant a legitimate claim to control of your data? It is a thorny question. Fortunately, we can decide to avoid answering it and instead choose to talk not about relinquishing control, but about exchanging value. Whatever the law may or may not require, people want to do business with companies—and with governments!—they can trust. In "real life," and, even more urgently, online, *trust* is a value added that confers a competitive edge on any merchant, organization, government agency, or nation that offers it as an integral aspect of a transaction. Instead of resorting to the Constitution, why not fall back on the free market? In commerce, more than ever before, transactional trust is as significant a value in pondering a purchase as low price, sexy design, or a ten-year warranty. In commerce as well as in diplomacy—the transactions between and among nations—trust is created through transparency of data control, and because trust is a highly competitive value, the compulsion of law or even international covenant is hardly necessary to enforce it. Sustainable profit—the transaction of fair value for fair value—is a powerful incentive to create the security necessary to privacy and the privacy security has always required.

Toward wide open secrecy

Although "Internet freedom" is no the silver bullet that will simultaneously slay tyranny and transform it into democracy, there can be no question that the United States must consistently face the world as both champion and evangelist of a free Internet—an Internet without censorship and unpolluted by egregiously covert surveillance and outright espionage. To become a worthy champion and evangelist, the United States must model for the nations of the world what it demands of those nations. It must achieve and exhibit transparent nationhood through a system of national government compatible with the cyberdiplomacy that a global Internet can both enable and ultimately must demand. Attaining this level of transparency requires creating a national mindset and culture shift capable of distinguishing truly necessary secrecy from superfluous and destructive opacity.

However the actions of Chelsea Manning, Edward Snowden, and WikiLeaks have impacted national security and security policy, they have beyond question challenged our notions of secrecy in the Internet age. They have brought to the fore the urgent need for policies of secrecy and surveillance "triage"—a policy and practice of determining what *really* needs to be secret and *really* needs to be tracked, and then distinguishing it from what does not.

Along with triage, the cases of Manning, Snowden, and WikiLeaks have made urgently apparent a corresponding need for an end to arbitrary opacity, which must be replaced by policies, procedures, laws, and technologies dedicated to perfecting and protecting what little secrecy is not only compatible with privacy, but necessary to both privacy and security. These questions and issues will be both subject and foundation of an effective cyberdiplomacy, a digitally enabled diplomacy compatible with and productive of what we may call wide open secrecy.

CHAPTER 5
DIGITAL CITADELS AND CYBER GUNBOATS

On November 9, 2016, the CIA reported to legislators that the United States intelligence community had concluded that Russia carried out cyberespionage operations during the 2016 election cycle to assist Donald J. Trump in defeating Hillary Clinton in the race for the presidency of the United States.[165] This news came after WikiLeaks published some 27,515 emails exfiltrated from computer systems of the Democratic National Committee (DNC) and emails from computers used by Clinton campaign chairman John Podesta. The emails were published in two batches, the first (19,252 emails) on July 22 and the second (8,263 emails) on November 6, 2016. Most were nondescript, routine communications, but some contained personally identifying information on political donors and others were revelations of embarrassing in-fighting, including evidence of DNC bias against the candidacy of Senator Bernie Sanders. Fallout from the emails resulted in the resignations of Representative Debbie Wasserman Schultz (D-FL) as DNC chair, DNC CEO Amy Dacey, DNC CFO Brad Marshall, and DNC Communications Director Luis Miranda. WikiLeaks denied having received the emails from Russian sources, and the Russian government, including President Vladimir Putin, denied responsibility for the hack.[166] The U.S. intelligence agencies reported that Russia also hacked Democratic House candidates as well as the Republican National Committee (RNC), but, in the case of the latter, kept the data, which (as of this writing in December 2016) has not been leaked or otherwise published.[167]

While the U.S. intelligence community rather quickly agreed on Russia as the source of the DNC hacks, there was initially difference of opinion on whether the hacks were intended more to influence the outcome of election or merely to undermine confidence in the results of the election. A *Washington Post* story published on December 16, 2016, however, revealed that the two main agencies, the FBI and the CIA, had reached definitive agreement that "Russia intervened in the 2016 election in part to help Donald Trump win the presidency."[168] Moreover, the Obama administration ascribed responsibility for the attacks to the "highest levels of the Russian government," presumably meaning Vladimir Putin himself.[169] Hillary Clinton went so far as say that the Russian attacks "were intended 'to undermine our democracy' and were ordered by Vladimir V. Putin 'because he has a personal beef against me.'"[170] For his part, both as a candidate and as president-elect, Donald J. Trump has repeatedly rejected the assertion that Russia was behind the attacks and even dismissed the CIA's attribution of that responsibility, pointing out that the CIA, in the run-up to the Iraq War, "are the same people that said Saddam Hussein had weapons of mass destruction." In a Fox News interview, he called the idea that Russia had helped him win "ridiculous. I think it's just another excuse. I don't believe it."[171] Critics of Trump have pointed out what *Mother Jones* and other news sources have called a "bromance" between the president-elect and the Russian autocrat.[172] The majority of federal elected officials, administrators, and U.S. political figures have accepted the hack into the U.S. elections as an act of Russian origin. When President Trump rocked the government by firing FBI Director James Comey, his staff and others in his administration released a variety of reasons for this step. But on May 11, 2017, he casually explained his motive to NBC News' anchor Lester Holt: "when I decided to just do it, I said to myself, I said, 'You know, this Russia thing with Trump and Russia is a made up story, it's an excuse by the Democrats for having lost an election that they should have won.'"[173] With that, congressional inquiries and a special counsel inquiry (under former FBI head Robert Mueller) were launched. As of late 2017, the investigations have catalogued a dizzying array of contacts between members of the Trump campaign and the Trump administration, on the one hand, and Kremlin-connected Russians on the other. While the issue of outright "collusion," "conspiracy," or "coordination" between the Trump campaign (or the Trump administration or Donald Trump personally) remains an open question as 2017 comes to a close, virtually no credible government or media figure doubts that Russia "meddled" in the 2016 presidential election.

War, cyberwar, and something else again
Some have even described the Russian "meddling" far more pointedly as

an "invasion" of the United States.[174] Invasion is, of course, an act of war, and back in 2007, when government-backed Russian hackers struck Estonia, NATO responded to its member's hour of need both earnestly and equivocally. It rushed to consider invoking Article 5 of the NATO treaty, the provision relating to "Collective defence," which holds that an attack against one member is to be deemed an attack against all members. NATO considered invoking collective defense, but soon backed down, the Estonian minister of defense explaining, "At present, NATO does not define cyber-attacks as a clear military action. This means that the provisions of Article V of the North Atlantic Treaty . . . will not automatically be extended to the attacked country."[175]

Without question, however, invasion is an act of war. To call the Russian hacks an "invasion" is therefore to call them acts of war. Has the ground shifted sufficiently since 2007 to legitimately consider as a genuine act of war a cyberattack aimed at influencing the outcome of an election, promoting one political candidate over another presumably to install a government more favorable to the attacker? Or is such an attack (to paraphrase Clausewitz) merely diplomacy by other means? I suggest that, in itself, the Russian cyberattack against the DNC was neither diplomacy nor warfare. It was an aggression somewhere between war and diplomacy. Indeed, contrary to the popular conception, diplomacy is not simply an alternative to military force. In part, diplomacy is founded on the hope of peaceful resolution, but, also in part, it is founded on all parties being mindful of the military consequences of the failure of peaceful resolution. This essential formulation should not be altered in the realm of cyberdiplomacy.

Few Americans, I believe, would advocate embarking on a *kinetic* war, a shooting war, in response to a *cyber*attack, even if it is described as an "invasion." Yet there is always the danger that cyberwarfare will escalate into kinetic warfare. This is less a fear when nations engage in mere cyberespionage. Presumably, espionage has been a regular feature of international relations since whenever we choose to deem the beginning of international relations. In the modern era, the Cold War saw the most pervasive and even institutionalized practice of espionage, but the collapse of the Soviet Union, which brought a "formal" end to the Cold War, has not brought an end to the espionage. We have learned to live with spying, and when U.S. authorities capture a spy, the government does not make war on the adversary who employed him or her.

In the case of cyber espionage, the danger of escalation increases greatly when the cyberattack is against, for instance, the Internet of Things (IoT). Consider the Stuxnet worm. Believed to have been jointly developed by Israel and the United States, Stuxnet has been called the world's first digital weapon. It is a sophisticated worm—malware that self-replicates to spread to other computers—first reported in June 2010, infiltrated into its target via a USB thumb drive or the equivalent rather than via the Internet, and designed to exploit unreported Windows vulnerabilities so that an attacker can gain control of a computer system. The purpose of Stuxnet was specifically to seek the presence of SCADA (Supervisory Control And Data Acquisition) software created by Siemens AG to control certain industrial equipment it manufactures. Introduced into a computer at the Natanz nuclear facility in Iran, Stuxnet issued commands to logic controllers regulating the centrifuges used to enrich uranium oxide in the process that creates fuel for a nuclear power plant or the core of a nuclear fission weapon. Via Stuxnet, agents (presumably from Israel and the U.S.) were able to rapidly raise and lower the speed of the centrifuge shafts, creating violent vibrations that destroyed the costly centrifuges, even while hiding these velocity variations from plant monitors. The operators of the Natanz plant would know what happened only after the damage had been done. The attack was carried out in November 2010 and destroyed about 10 percent of Natanz's 10,000 centrifuges, seriously impeding enriched uranium production in Iran.[176]

Stuxnet was arguably an act of war—not just cyberwarfare, but of cyberwarfare used to produce the kind of damage previously created by kinetic weapons, as (for example) in Operation Opera (a/k/a Operation Babylon), the 1981 Israeli surprise air strike against a nuclear reactor under construction outside of Baghdad, Iraq.[177]

Whether a state-sponsored cross-border cyberattack is directed against the IoT to produce the kind of physical result formerly created by overt acts of kinetic warfare or is a PSYOPS (psychological warfare) operation (sometimes euphemistically labeled as an act of "public diplomacy") intended to influence an election, it is open to interpretation as a hostile invasion. So interpreted, it becomes an act of war that conceivably warrants and justifies an act of war in response. Whether kinetic or psychological in effect, the potential for cyberwarfare to escalate into kinetic warfare is significant.

Can we have a cyberwar treaty?

There are many good arguments to be made for creating and opening for global signature a cyberwar treaty to define just how and when *cyberwar* becomes *war*, plain and simple, and to define agreed-upon international norms that might avert such an escalation.[178] Nevertheless, the arguments for skepticism concerning such a treaty are also compelling. The nearest existing precedent or parallel to an international convention on cyberwar is the Convention on Cybercrime, which the Council of Europe (COE) opened for signature on November 23, 2001, and which entered into force on July 1, 2004. As of December 2016, fifty states have ratified the convention and are party to it (and another five have signed, but not yet ratified, it).[179] The convention establishes a "a common criminal policy aimed at the protection of society against cybercrime."[180] This is an entirely laudable purpose; however, the convention places a number requirements on signatories, many of which are onerous in that they require a significant compromise of traditional national sovereignty. For instance, signatories are required to "adopt legislation banning various computer crimes, including illegal access and interception, data and system interference, misuse of devices, forgery, fraud, child pornography, and intellectual property offenses." They must also "adopt laws concerning the investigation of computer-related crimes" and must agree to "cooperate in the investigation and prosecution of such crimes with other countries (i.e., via extradition and mutual law-enforcement assistance)."[181] In response to these conditions, signatories created "'consensus' on computer crimes only by adopting vague definitions that are subject to different interpretations by different states. Even with vague definitions, many nations conditioned their consent on declarations and reservations (the United States had more than a half dozen) that further diluted the scope of covered crimes, making the treaty's obligations even less uniform and less demanding." As for the mutual assistance obligations in the prevention, interdiction, and prosecution of cybercrime, the "duty to cooperate contains large loopholes for requests that prejudice such essential interests as national sovereignty and security." Indeed, a signatory may reject cooperation on the widest of grounds, and the convention lacks any enforcement mechanism. "The Cybercrime Convention experience teaches that nations significantly disagree about what digital practices should be outlawed and are deeply skeptical about even the weakest forms of international cooperation in this area. It is a cautionary tale for those who believe in the feasibility of a broader cybersecurity treaty involving more nations and covering more ambitious topics that bear a closer relationship to sovereignty and national security.[182]

If the cybercrime convention has proved to be disappointing, what reason is there to believe that a cyberwar convention will fare much better?

Diplomacy is rightly viewed as an alternative to the violence of war. Nevertheless, the effectiveness of diplomacy rests on the threat of consequences if diplomatic agreements are breached, and the consequences often include war. Although it is an alternative to war, diplomacy is in significant measure founded on war. I suggest, therefore, that any meaningful cyberdiplomacy must be founded not on hopeful but unenforceable global conventions, but on a transparent collective regime of cyber defense as well as more aggressive *active* cyber defense, a posture just short of preemptive offense.

Let us begin with collective cyber defense. On December 5, 2012, the U.S. House of Representatives approved a May 30 Senate resolution opposing "the proposals, in . . . the United Nations General Assembly, the United Nations Commission on Science and Technology for Development, and the International Telecommunication Union, [that] would justify under international law increased government control over the Internet." In short, Congress voted to keep Internet control out of UN hands.[183] It was the appropriate thing to do. After all, the Preamble to the Charter of the United Nations establishes the world body not on the authority of the governments of the world but in the name of "we the peoples of the United Nations," and it announces among the UN's purposes the employment of "international machinery for the promotion of the economic and social advancement of all peoples." Among the UN's many agencies, one, the International Telecommunications Union (ITU), founded as the International Telegraph Union in 1865 and incorporated into the UN in 1947, is responsible for the coordination, standardization, and promotion of the global Internet. Nevertheless, its mandate is clearly technical in nature and addresses issues to ensure global interoperabilty and to "bridge the digital divide" by "expanding access to ICTs [information and communications technologies] globally," which, according to the ITU website, "is in everybody's interest." The Preamble to the Constitution of the ITU "fully recognize[es] the sovereign right of each State to regulate its telecommunication" while also seeking to foster "international cooperation among peoples and economic and social development by means of efficient telecommunication services."[184] Through the ITU, the United Nations claims a legitimate role in global ICT, including the Internet. But, just as clearly, the UN role must be primarily technical (the Internet is part of the "international machinery for . . . the advancement of all peoples") with the added mission of expanding access. In 2012, however, some member nations proposed regulatory authority that violates both the UN Charter and the ITU Constitution by making the international community complicit with governments and regimes that may seek to, in effect, "rewire" the Internet by cutting off their citizens' access to data and communication and by patrolling Internet content and communication, censoring information, suppressing bottom-up Internet constituents and political and cultural institutions, and imposing taxes and other restrictive charges on international communication. It was against this that Congress stood firm, especially since the UN discussions had been conducted, uncharacteristically, in secret, behind closed doors.

Looking to NATO

Neither the U.S. nor the EU wants to give any government the authority to manipulate or censor the flow or the content of data across the global Internet. Even less do they relish the prospect of the United Nations being used as an instrument to sanction such control. The safest, most effective, and ultimately freest means of collectively defending the Internet and its connected nations against cyberwar is not through the ITU or the United Nations. I believe that an alliance of nations is required for effective collective defense. We have the foundation of such an alliance already in place. It is of long standing, and it has a proven historical track record. It is NATO.[185]

In 1999, at the height of its military success during its intervention in the Kosovo War (1998-1999), NATO issued *The Alliance's Strategic Concept*, a document published on April 24 that codified, in sixty-five numbered articles, what NATO leaders called an "out-of-area" strategy.[186] Acknowledging that the fall of the Soviet Union had transformed the global threat picture from a bipolar antagonism between two superpowers (with Western Europe in the middle) to something far more complex (multipolar), NATO redefined its "territory" to encompass any place on the planet that presented new threats to Euro-Atlantic security. Even more profoundly, the enlargement of NATO's mission was not just an enlargement of geographical scope, but of conceptual scope. During the Cold War, "armed aggression" was quite easy to define. It was Soviet tanks rolling out of the East. The Balkans conflict (also called the Yugoslav Wars, 1991-2001) demonstrated that a military threat could be far more diffuse, consisting of aggressions motivated by religion, ethics, even quasi-tribal affiliation and such acts as torture, rape, "ethnic cleansing" (genocide), and the creation of a massive refugee exodus. Instead of a cross-border conflict, the threat could be a civil war with regional consequences. Enlarging the concept even further, the threat might be proliferation of weapons of mass destruction and terrorism sponsored not by states, but by political, ethnic, or religious groups or even by individuals.

Like other crises before it, the Balkans conflict suddenly injected new relevance into NATO, spurring the adoption of the "out-of-area" strategy, which had the potential of sustaining NATO's relevance far beyond the Cold War. In 1999, the very year that the new strategy was adopted, two Chinese air force colonels, Qiao Liang and Wang Xiangsui, published a book known in English as *Unrestricted Warfare.* The authors argued that the "age of technological integration and globalization," the age of the Internet just then emerging, had "realigned the relationship of weapons to war, while the appearance of weapons of new concepts, and particularly new concepts of weapons, [had] gradually blurred the face of war." In all ages past, war was defined exclusively by the use of armed force. Now, the Chinese colonels asked, "Does a single 'hacker' attack count as a hostile act or not? Can using financial instruments to destroy a country's economy be seen as a battle?"[187]

Attempting to answer such questions using the traditional definitions of war, the authors warned, means they will remain unanswerable. "When we suddenly realize that all these non-war actions may be the new factors constituting future warfare, we have to come up with a new name for this new form of war: Warfare which transcends all boundaries and limits, in short: unrestricted warfare."[188]

The 1999 NATO *Strategic Concept* makes no mention of cyberwarfare, and we have no evidence that NATO leaders were even aware of Qiao and Wang's book. Nevertheless, as *Unrestricted Warfare* predicted, cyberspace would increasingly figure as a battlespace for what Qiao and Wang called "war in which information technology is used to obtain or suppress information." In such a war, "there is nothing . . . that cannot become a weapon"; therefore, "our understanding of weapons must have an awareness that breaks through all boundaries." A "single man-made stock-market crash, a single computer virus invasion, or a single rumor or scandal that results in a fluctuation in the enemy country's exchange rates or exposes the leaders of an enemy country on the Internet, all can be included in the ranks of new-concept weapons," weapons "that are closely linked to the lives of the common people." The "digital fighter is taking over the role formerly played by the 'blood and iron' warrior," so that "warfare is no longer . . . an exclusive imperial garden where professional soldiers alone can mingle."[189]

Cyberwarfare is the ultimate "out-of-area" mission space. The "out-of-area" concept that was the key to NATO's enduring relevance in 1999 remains today the key that opens a profound role for NATO in cyberspace. As noted earlier in this book, NATO considered but ultimately rejected invoking Article 5, on "collective defense," as a mandate for member nations to come to the aid of Estonia when it fell under Russian cyberattack in 2007. Nevertheless, NATO *did respond* to the attack—by planning cyber defenses for itself and its members. A NATO policy on cyber defense was quickly approved in January 2008 and was endorsed in April at the Bucharest Summit.[190] On May 14, 2008,

Estonia, Germany, Italy, Latvia, Lithuania, Slovak Republic, and Spain signed a Memorandum of Understanding formally establishing the Cooperative Cyber Defense Centre of Excellence (CCDCOE) in Tallinn. The North Atlantic Council fully accredited the CCDCOE in October, and both Turkey and the United States signed on before the end of 2008. Other members joined between 2010 and 2013. The CCDCOE had been conceived as early as 2004 and became initially operational that year—with a core staff of ten Estonian experts—but it was the 2007 cyberattacks that provided the impetus to create a permanent international cyber center.

By no means is the Cooperative Cyber Defense Centre of Excellence (CCDCOE) capable of fighting a cyberwar. Although permanently established, it was described in 2011 as an "embryonic" organization with about thirty full-time staff members. To put this in perspective, in 2011 NATO had a budget of about $7 billion and employed, on a permanent basis, fourteen thousand military and civilian staff personnel. The latter number does not count troops deployed on missions, since these personnel are soldiers, sailors, airmen, and marines contributed by member states as needed. It is notoriously difficult to obtain accurate budget figures for NATO, and it has not been possible to obtain budget information for the CCDCOE, but, compared to the rest of NATO, we can safely assume that it is, if not vanishingly small, at least vanishingly modest. The CCDCOE's mission, as currently stated, is relatively minimal:

> To enhance the capability, cooperation and information sharing among NATO, NATO nations and partners in cyber defence by virtue of education, research and development, lessons learned and consultation. Our vision is to be the main source of expertise in the field of cooperative cyber defence by accumulating, creating, and disseminating knowledge in related matters within NATO, NATO nations and partners.[191]

As a clearinghouse and educational resource rather than a cyber army, CCDCOE is, in fact, a humble undertaking. This was the case in 2011 and remains the case in 2016. Its authority and capability are severely limited. For one thing, we need to bear in mind that NATO still does not define cyberattack as an "armed attack." For another, the CCDCOE functions within NATO's institutional limits. These include funding shortfalls, as EU countries persist in spending less on alliance-related defense than they had promised, and the necessity of undertaking no mission or any other significant action without a consensus of the membership. And, by "consensus," NATO means unanimity. One objector—a single holdout—can and will block NATO military action. Assuming NATO members agree that a particular cyberattack constitutes a clear armed attack (and they have yet to agree on this), the need for consensus on any proposed response makes it difficult, perhaps impossible, to respond quickly to a cyberattack.

Although NATO has yet to equate *cyberattack* with *armed attack* (the trigger for invocation of Article 5), the North Atlantic Treaty also offers Article 4: "The Parties will consult together whenever, in the opinion of any of them, the territorial integrity, political independence or security of any of the Parties is threatened."[192] The perception of a *threat* represents a much lower threshold for action than the "armed attack" specified in Article 5. For this reason, a threat may be more successful in galvanizing NATO members to act jointly. Nevertheless, acting preemptively—as against a threat—still may require the kind of rapid action for which NATO's decision-making apparatus is structurally unsuited.

Given the context of budgetary, institutional, and structural limitations in which CCDCOE operates, it has—perhaps wisely, perhaps simply inevitably—put itself at the core of a concept of cyber defense that is more about hardening cyber infrastructure and improving cyber practices than it is about responding to attacks. This approach puts CCDCOE in line with NATO's longstanding role as a source of military standards and best practices—all of which, however, are voluntary, since each NATO member ultimately determines the scope and limits of its share in any NATO mission or initiative.

Modest, small, downright "embryonic," existing in a culture of limitation, the CCDCOE has nevertheless established, on a global scale, thought leadership in cyber security and cyber defense. What is more, it has done so more boldly, thoroughly, and openly than any other military alliance or, for that matter, multinational organization of any kind. It leverages a small permanent staff and a paltry budget to create a source of thought leadership in cyber security and cyber defense unavailable from any other collective or collaborative source. It offers authoritative and innovative research publications on such topics as "Peacetime Regime for State Activities in Cyberspace" (a "multi-disciplinary approach to the technical, legal, policy and diplomacy aspects of State activities in cyberspace during peacetime"), "Strategic Cyber Security" (which takes computer security from a technical discipline to a strategic concept), "The Virtual Battlefield" (a high-level exploration of all aspects of cyberwarfare), "International Cyber Incidents: Legal Considerations," and "Frameworks for International Cybersecurity" ("a compilation of cyber security legal and policy instruments adopted by the

Council of Europe, the European Union, the Group of Eight, the International Telecommunication Union, the Organization for Economic Co-Operation and Development, the Organization for Cooperation and Security in Europe and the United Nations that provide various tools and approaches to handle the threats against modern information societies").[193]

In addition, CCDCOE publishes proceedings from its conferences and workshops, which gather experts from both inside and outside the alliance to make presentations on subjects in law, policy, strategy and technology. A major program within the conference and workshop series is CyCon, the International Conference on Cyber Conflict, which discusses trends in cybersecurity. The 2013 CyCon addressed the cutting-edge issues relating to the technical, strategic and legal implications of using automatic methods to manage cyber conflicts.[194]

CCDCOE also conducts cyber defense exercises, including real-time network defense exercises designed to help participants acquire the skills needed to fend off a real attack. CCDCOE contributes to the planning, development, and execution of the NATO Cyber Defence Exercise (Cyber Coalition), which is "designed to give its participants a better understanding of NATO's Cyber Defence capabilities and to identify areas for improvement within the NATO-wide Cyber Defence community."[195]

In addition to designing and conducting exercises, the Centre offers a variety of courses and seminars in awareness, technology (including Cyber Defense Monitoring and Security Events Management; Botnet Mitigation Training; Introductory Forensics Training; IT Systems Attacks and Defense; and Malware and Exploits Essentials), and international law as it relates to cyber operations.

Without doubt, the single most important of the Centre's thought-leading publications is *The National Cyber Security Framework Manual,* also known as the *Tallinn Manual.*[196] It is a bold move toward defining NATO member national cyberwarfare policy and doctrine and providing a framework for international cooperation in cybersecurity and cyber defense among NATO members. Even more significantly, it sets out a framework for national cybersecurity and cyber defense standards. These it unambiguously calls "national mandates," investing the moral capital of the alliance in a bid to convince members of their ethical obligation to define, meet, and maintain NATO standards of cybersecurity and cyber defense. As with the rest of NATO's standards and initiatives, this is not an incursion into the sovereignty of members, but it is the application of moral suasion, and the CCDCOE functions to develop models for the national mandates.

At the heart of the *Tallinn Manual* is a call not only to member governments to rally to the common defense of cyberspace, but also to the private sector, which encompasses enterprises that are increasingly global and multinational. As with cyberspace and cyberwar, today's business knows no borders and is confined by no sovereignties. The *Tallinn Manual* identifies "critical infrastructure protection (CIP)" as "the catch-all term that seeks to involve the providers of essential services of a country within a national security framework." Acknowledging that "most of the service providers (such as public utilities, finance or telecommunications) are in the private sector," the manual defines the necessity of extending "government support to help protect [private sector companies] and the essential services they provide from modern threats."

In this, NATO again takes the lead by daring to proclaim a truth that many in the United States, including a controlling bloc of legislators, find inconvenient and persistently refuse to accept: As cyberspace and thus cyberwar cannot be bounded by national borders, so they cannot be contained exclusively in the public or the private sector. Cyberspace is, above all, absolutely permeable. Accordingly, the *Tallinn Manual* offers at least the outline of a framework for creating a productive relationship between private and public sectors in cyber security and cyber defense. It recognizes private sector companies as "stewards" of the national and global Internet and therefore provides the foundation of a definition of a cyber security "mandate" for the private sector, regardless of corporate nationality.

Cybersecurity and cyber defense figure with increasing prominence throughout NATO, not just within the CCDCOE. Article 49 of the "Chicago Summit Declaration," issued by the "Heads of State and Government participating in the meeting of the North Atlantic Council in Chicago on 20 May 2012," acknowledged that "Cyber attacks continue to increase significantly in number and evolve in sophistication and complexity" and noted that in 2011, the alliance, meeting in Lisbon, adopted a "Cyber Defence Concept, Policy, and Action Plan, which are now being implemented." NATO's own network and computer infrastructure were well on their way to being brought "under centralised cyber protection, to ensure that enhanced cyber defence capabilities protect our collective investment in NATO." Article 49 pledged to "further integrate cyber defence measures into Alliance structures and procedures and, as individual nations, [to] remain committed to identifying and delivering national cyber defence capabilities that strengthen Alliance collaboration and interoperability, including through NATO defence planning processes."[197]

The ongoing cyber agenda included further developing the ability of NATO and NATO members "to prevent, detect, defend against, and recover from cyber attacks." The NATO members agreed to "address the cyber security threats and to improve our common security" and to engage not only with "relevant partner nations on a case-by-case basis," but also "with international organisations, inter alia the EU, as agreed, the Council of Europe, the UN and the OSCE, in order to increase concrete cooperation." Finally, all members resolved to "take full advantage of the expertise offered by the Cooperative Cyber Defence Centre of Excellence in Estonia."[198]

While Article 49 of the Chicago Declaration principally addressed the military aspects of cybersecurity, which were detailed further on NATO's website, an article published in *Joint Forces Quarterly* a year before the Chicago meeting indicates the even larger direction in which the cybersecurity and cyberdefense mission may take NATO. Titled "Estonia: Cyber Window into the future of NATO," and written by Häly Laasme, an Estonian policy analyst, the article reviews the 2007 cyberattack on Estonia and how it gave rise to the CCDCOE. Laasme suggests that this small NATO center represents a venture for the alliance beyond the military sector.[199]

Moreover, Laasme explains that CCDCOE is a source of cyber defense and security standards and best practices for military, civilian government, and private sectors, and implies that it is even more: the first step toward a new future for NATO. "Europe," he writes, "needs a new action plan for making the best use of information and communication technologies (ICT) to speed up economic recovery and lay the foundations of a sustainable digital future." And Laasme lists seven priority areas for a European "Digital Agenda," including creating a Digital Single Market, improving borderless interoperability between ICT products and services, boosting Internet trust and security, creating faster Internet access, encouraging investment in R&D, enhancing digital literacy, skills, and inclusion, and "applying ICT to address social challenges such as climate change, rising health care costs, and aging populations."[200]

Obviously, Laasme does not propose that NATO be charged with achieving, on its own, all seven priorities, none of which are directly let alone principally military in nature; and yet he places this discussion in the middle of an essay subtitled, "Cyber Window into the Future of NATO." As cyberspace and all activities conducted in cyberspace (war, business, education, civilization) irresistibly permeate all borders and sectorial boundaries, so a "military" alliance moving into cybersecurity and cyber defense must assume a borderless and unbounded role in cyberspace. NATO's footprint in cyberspace, if it is to continue to grow, necessitates a future for the alliance beyond the confines of military matters for the simple reason that activities in cyberspace cannot be confined.

Enlarging NATO's role in cybersecurity will put the alliance at the very center of addressing one of most serious military and economic threats facing its members—and, for that matter, facing most of the world. This centrality would not only be analogous to NATO's leadership role during the Cold War, it would be commensurate with it. Yet the new *cyber* role will be far less expensive and far less provocative than NATO's exclusively military role in the fifty-year-long postwar conflict. Even considered from a narrowly military perspective, defense and security operations in cyberspace are less costly—in both treasure and lives—than kinetic defense and security operations in physical space. Moreover, the cyber role has the potential to unify states rather than divide them, with respect to NATO and non-NATO members alike. The security of the Internet is a benefit globally, without the zero-sum economic and territorial implications of most kinetic military actions undertaken in physical space.

To those who fear that a NATO cyber role will militarize the Internet, two responses may be offered. First, China, Russia, North Korea, Iran, and a handful of non-state actors (including ISIL) have already militarized the Internet. Cyberspace is now unquestionably a battlespace. Second, NATO's presence in cyber affairs will not be exclusively military. As Häly Laasme suggested in 2011, it will also be economic, political, and ethical.

Even though NATO operations are typically sanctioned by the United Nations, with which the alliance has a strong historical and operational relationship, a NATO that functions as the center of cybersecurity and cyber defense offers a far more desirable alternative to an Internet that is "regulated" by the UN's International Telecommunications Union (ITU). Moving from the short- and mid-term impact of a NATO role in cybersecurity and cyber defense to the longer-term perspective, we can expect that using the cyber mission to create a newly relevant NATO will drive the continued and politically desirable geopolitical expansion of the alliance. As Zbigniew Brezezinski remarked in 2008, "NATO . . . has the experience, the institutions, and the means to eventually become the hub of a globe-spanning web of various regional cooperative-security undertakings among states with the growing power to act."[201]

Finally, in the more distant long term, as the "hub" of a "security web," NATO can even work to revitalize the United Nations, an institution in need of "rebranding" perhaps even more urgently than

NATO. "The resulting security web would fill a need that the United Nations by itself cannot meet, but from which the UN system will actually benefit," Brezezinski wrote. "In pursuing that strategic mission, NATO would not only be preserving transatlantic political unity; it would also be responding to the twenty-first century's novel and increasingly urgent security agenda."[202] By accepting and developing international leadership in cybersecurity and cyber defense, NATO, as a guarantor of cybersecurity, will expand its scope to encompass service as the center of an economic, political, and ethical alliance. To the degree that NATO succeeds in achieving this position among its members, it may also step beyond the confines of the particular alliance (no matter how expansive those "confines" may be) to become an institution that serves the entire world by protecting the Internet, the greatest, most expansive civilization-enabling infrastructure in history.

As NATO served throughout the Cold War as collective defense alliance and a military platform for diplomacy, so it could serve the same functions in cyber defense and cyberdiplomacy. The current NATO Centres of Excellence, through which NATO administers and coordinates its cyber defense programs,[203] can serve as the core of what we might call *digital citadels,* centers equipped to respond to cyber threats and cyberattacks as well as to share best practices and specific technologies to prevent cyberattack. Indeed, Russia's Internet-based election "meddling" may provide a Cold War-like motive for backing NATO cyberdefense authority and capability. In the digital realm, the geopolitical environment seems to be getting repolarized—with Russia clearly forming one of the poles. Moreover, the Trump administration has shown interest in strengthening national cybersecurity, which has prompted the president's cybersecurity advisors to resign, citing the president's "'insufficient attention' to threats."[204] The United States may need all the help it can get.

Cyber gunboat diplomacy

But conducting cyberdiplomacy from a platform of strength requires more than digital citadels. It also calls for the capability of a more aggressive *active defense* system, for which we may draw on the language of traditional diplomacy. "Gunboat diplomacy" is a term that originated in the nineteenth century to describe the means by which relatively powerful states intimidated relatively less powerful states into granting whatever concessions were desired. Often, intimidation would take the form of a military display, as when President Theodore Roosevelt sent the United States Navy's battle fleet—the so-called Great White Fleet of sixteen white-hulled battleships and supporting vessels—

on a circumnavigation of the globe from December 16, 1907 to February 22, 1909. The objective was to impress the world.

It did.

An active cyber defense calls for *cyber gunboats* in addition to digital citadels—in short, a retaliatory capacity in addition to more or less passive defenses. We must be willing to retaliate, in cyberspace, against state actors who attack us in cyberspace. Targeting the aggressor's financial sector can be effective, but we must be willing and able to simultaneously compromise the aggressor's military cyber infrastructure, especially its command and control systems. This may be critical to preventing or at least degrading a kinetic response to our cyber retaliation.

In the best case, developing a powerful fleet of cyber gunboats will create a world in which we never actually have to deploy them in war. If our adversaries are convinced that an attack on our cyber assets will result in a massive retaliation against theirs, they should be deterred from such action. This is, of course, an analogy to the Cold War–era nuclear warfare concept of mutually assured destruction (MAD): the doctrine that no adversary will launch a nuclear first strike against a nation that is publicly committed to retaliating in kind. MAD was undeniably successful in averting thermonuclear war during the long Cold War period and beyond. Against adversary states that have highly developed digital networks, it is likely that MAD will prove an effective historical precedent on which to negotiate peaceful diplomatic solutions to cyber-related disputes; however, the application of the deterrence concept to aggressive cyber defense tends to break down in inverse proportion to the level of an adversary's digital infrastructure. The more asymmetric the relation between defender and adversary—that is, the greater the defender's digital assets versus those of the adversary—the less effective MAD will be. An adversary relatively poor in cyber assets presents relatively few targets for cyber retaliation. Moreover, such an adversary may launch cyberattacks on the assumption that it has little or nothing to lose from cyber retaliation.

Consider the case of North Korea. Recent anxiety concerning the hostility of this rogue state has understandably centered on the nuclear (and perhaps thermonuclear) threat it presents.[205] We must not let this kinetic threat, terrifying though it may be, blind us to North Korea's demonstrated and growing weaponization of the Internet and global digital connectivity.[206] The nation has invested relatively little in a civilian power grid and civilian Internet infrastructure. (Everyone is familiar with those nocturnal satellite photographs that show the dazzling lights below the DMZ and near total darkness above it.) Nevertheless,

North Korea's military possesses significant (though not world-class) *offensive* cyberwarfare capacity. For instance, South Korean officials attributed cyberattacks against three banks and the nation's two largest broadcasters on March 20, 2013, to North Korea. And in 2009, just before Washington government offices closed for the July 4 holiday break, North Korean agents unleashed a botnet DDoS attack from some 40,000 infected computers worldwide. In the U.S., the Department of Homeland Security and Department of State websites, suddenly swamped with pings, became temporarily unavailable. Next, between July 4 and July 9, websites belonging to the Department of the Treasury, U.S. Secret Service, Federal Trade Commission, and Department of Transportation were all periodically shut down. The New York Stock Exchange, NASDAQ, and New York Mercantile Exchange were hit and temporarily disabled, as was the *Washington Post.* The U.S. government has never officially attributed the attacks to North Korea, but South Korean officials have not demurred. South Korea's National Intelligence Service (NIS) identified a North Korean hacker unit, known as Lab 110, as the source.[207]

There are effective defensive steps that can be taken to thwart the effects of DDoS attacks such as those launched by North Korea in 2009. Richard Clarke points out that, while several government and financial sites were indeed temporarily brought down, attacks against the White House website failed because, in 1999, when he served on the National Security Council as National Coordinator for Security, Infrastructure Protection, and Counter-terrorism, Clarke "had arranged with a company known as Akamai to route traffic seeking the White House website to the nearest of over 20,000 servers scattered throughout the world." Thus, when the North Korean attack hit in 2009, only "servers nearest the source of the attacker" were affected. While the "White House website in Asia had trouble," no other White House site suffered.[208] Even the attacks against other government and financial industry websites were fairly rapidly contained and controlled. The problem is that current U.S. military doctrine puts little emphasis on defensive measures—the digital citadels that might be developed under NATO—and relies instead on offense and the retaliatory threat. Against states such as North Korea (with a well-developed offensive cyber capability, but an infrastructure that relies remarkably little on a cyber-connected grid) and non-state actors (let's call them terrorist hackers), the threat of cyber retaliation strikes no fear and therefore creates little or no deterrence. In terms of cyber infrastructure, North Korea, much like a non-state terrorist group, has little or nothing to lose. After all, the nation's lights are already out. A U.S. first strike may provoke cyber retaliation against which we have inadequate defense. Moreover, in the absence of an adequate cyber defense, military offensive capabilities may be rendered inoperative or even turned against us. Should the U.S. offensive posture fail to deter cyberattacks, the imperative will be strong to respond to a serious cyberattack with a kinetic attack, thereby instantly escalating cyberwar into a shooting war.

Both passive defense and aggressive active defense—digital citadels *and* cyber gunboats—are necessary to provide adequate defense against cyberwar, but neither alone is sufficient. And if neither alone is sufficient for credible cyber defense, neither alone is sufficient as a military platform from which effective cyberdiplomacy can be conducted. The United States Cyber Command (USCYBERCOM), charged with organizing cyber resources and coordinating the defense of U.S. military networks, is primarily an offensive force. It also leaves undefended civilian, private-sector cyber networks, many of which are connected to critical national infrastructure. For that matter, the computer network of the Democratic National Committee was the civilian, private-sector target through which a state aggressor, Russia, sought to disrupt and/or influence the 2016 U.S. presidential election. Although directed at a civilian network, this was arguably an act of war against the United States. To create a stronger platform of national cyber defense—and thus a more effective platform for cyberdiplomacy—the defense of all U.S. digital infrastructure should be closely coordinated under some authority. Probably the best solution is to make USCYBERCOM responsible for coordinating all cyber defense. As for USCYBERCOM's current offensive function, this should be institutionally integrated into NATO as the basis for a more aggressive active defense component of collective defense.

Cyber defense cannot be defined by national borders. It cries out to be integrated into an effective alliance for transnational defense. Such collective defense, with offensive retaliatory capability, will enable NATO allies to conduct cyberdiplomacy from a position of collective strength. Since the digital, economic, and cultural networks among the NATO nations are so extensive, intensive, pervasive, and vital, the coordination and collectivization of both the military and diplomatic dimensions of cyber is not only desirable, but imperative.

CHAPTER 6
INFRASTRUCTURES

"Conventional" diplomacy, diplomacy in the predigital era, developed as a profession and as a set of codified norms after the rise of the nation-state in the late sixteenth century beginning with the emergence of the Dutch Republic. Between the sixteenth and nineteenth centuries, the physical, cultural, political, and legal infrastructures of the nation-state became culturally and politically institutionalized. Diplomacy in this predigital era evolved in an environment that was both thoroughly defined and thoroughly established.

This is hardly the case with cyberdiplomacy. Every aspect of our hyperconnected world has evolved with extraordinary speed. The result remains soft and uncertain, like poured cement that has yet to cure. In the United States, for example, 67.7 percent of the 2012 population were born before the emergence of the Internet.[209] In other words, more than two-thirds of the population was born and came of age before the political, economic, and cultural infrastructure of the world was defined by global digital networks. This means that cyberdiplomacy has been emerging into an environment that is still very much in the process of becoming. Much is undefined and far from certain. In fact, we know just four things:

1. A world marked in great measure by pervasive digital connection requires a diplomacy significantly, even profoundly, different from a world that is not so marked.
2. Cyberdiplomacy must necessarily differ from pre-digital diplomacy.
3. Our global digital infrastructures (physical, political, cultural,

economic) are evolving and are therefore fluid. The evolution is rapid, but the end is not in sight and has not yet been persuasively imagined. We are far from certain of what our digital infrastructures currently are, and we don't know what they will become.

4. Cyberdiplomacy is therefore evolving and fluid. We are far from certain of what cyperdiplomacy is, and we don't know what it will become.

The technological infrastructure

As mentioned in chapter 3, we are not well-served by the popular term *cyberspace,* an ethereal, other-dimensional label we casually apply to something that is not a "space," a void, but the product of physical things, an infrastructure of power generating plants, hardwired electrical grids, fiber-connected communication grids, cables, digital processors of all kinds, which can and mostly are owned, operated, and controlled by governments and by companies that typically have allegiance or interest in governments. We often think of the Internet as essentially borderless. To a significant but varying degree this is true, but it is also true, as discussed in chapter three, that (for example) Internet data enters and leaves China at relatively few points, each of which is regulated by sophisticated gateway router systems. Beyond the ability of states to use specific items of hardware to monitor, filter, censor, and block cross-border Internet traffic, there is also the vulnerabilities all physical structures share. Every part parts of the communications grid, the technological infrastructure of this fiction we conjure up by the term "cyberspace," can break—or be broken.

The first transatlantic telegraph cable was completed in 1858. Technological marvel though it was, the cable very quickly failed due mainly to the rapid deterioration of insulation in saltwater. The lesson here was that the seemingly ineffable miracle of electrical communication was literally grounded in a dirty and destructive physical reality. Trans-border, transcontinental connectivity proved to be fragile. Although the fragility eventually yielded to improved engineering, cable sabotage "was common during both World Wars." In the Cold War, the Soviets probably tampered with the trans-Atlantic Cable off Newfoundland, and the U.S. Navy certainly deployed divers from submarines to physically tap into Soviet military communication in Operation Ivy Bells. But even non-nefarious activities remain a menace to the trans-oceanic cables. Such things as "dropped anchors and fishing nets" account for "about 60 percent of cut cable incidents."[210]

Little remembered today, Operation Ivy Bells is worth recalling. It began in the 1970s, only to end abruptly in 1981 when an NSA employee, Ronald Pelton, sold Ivy Bells information to the Soviets for $35,000.[211] The betrayal of Ivy Bells did not discourage later tapping of the undersea portion of the Internet's "backbone" by the United States and, presumably, other powers. Before we go into this further, we need to know that the *backbone* is the trunk line of the Internet. In the United States, for example, hundreds of Internet service providers (ISPs) operate, but only about seven (experts vary slightly on the exact number) are deemed "Tier 1 ISPs." They control the backbone with which the smaller ISPs connect and from which their networks branch. The Tier 1 backbone consists of hundreds of thousands of miles of fiber optic cable bundles, the overland portion of which connects at the shoreline to undersea fiber optic cables.

As incredibly complex as the Internet is, its backbone is starkly simple—simple and vulnerable to both digital and physical attack. An attacker bent on compromising, disrupting, or disabling the Internet in any extensive way must target the backbone, which, as reported in a 2015 article in the *MIT Technology Review*, "is disturbingly easy to attack." Doing so successfully could "block access to a major online service like YouTube, or to intercept online communications on a vast scale."[212] The authors of the article cite "long-standing weaknesses in the protocol that works out how to route data across the different networks making up the Internet. Almost all the infrastructure running that protocol does not even use a basic security technology that would make it much harder to block or intercept data." This technology is available, but it is not being used, presumably (as Wim Remes of the security company Rapid7 explains) because there is "limited probability of these attacks"; however, he points out, "the impact once they happen is huge." The significant weakness is in the border gateway protocol (BGP), which is employed by the large routers of the Tier 1 ISPs (among others) "to figure out how to get data [from the backbone] to different places." BGP lacks "security mechanisms ... to verify the information they are receiving or the identity of the routers providing it."[213]

Just as the fragility of undersea cable communications has been known since the inception of such technology, so the BGP vulnerability has been common knowledge among security experts for decades. One security company, Qrator, even recently demonstrated that "BGP could be manipulated to obtain a security certificate in the name of a particular website without permission, making it possible to impersonate [the website] and decrypt secured traffic."[214] Yet because of a consensus among ISPs that an attack on the BGP is unlikely, the vulnerability remains largely unaddressed.

Just how serious would such an attack be? Nobody knows, but most experts believe that the Internet is so widely distributed that even attacking the BGP, while highly disruptive, would probably not bring down the entire global network.

But could an attacker strike even more deeply into the backbone? The answer is yes, and the consequences would be far graver. The target of choice for anyone who wants to massively disrupt the global Internet remains the undersea cables, which carry 99 percent of all transoceanic digital communication. Indeed, on October 25, 2015, Pentagon officials reported concern that Russian submarines and "spy ships" were "aggressively operating near the vital undersea cables." This raised "concerns among some American military and intelligence officials that the Russians might be planning to attack those lines in times of tension or conflict."[215]

The simplest attack would be by brute kinetic force. A submarine would place and detonate an explosive charge near a cable to blast it apart and sever it. But NSA contractor Edward Snowden, through material he leaked via WikiLeaks and interviews published in *The Guardian, Washington Post, Der Spiegel,* and *The New York Times,* revealed a subtler approach. The GCHQ (Government Communications Headquarters) of the British government and the NSA of the United States government (Snowden's leaks revealed) operated collaboratively to tap virtually all digital data traveling through undersea cables. The volume of intercepts is staggering. A single British program, called Tempora, acquired approximately 21 million gigabytes per day. Snowden's revelations about the NSA PRISM/US-984XN program have drawn far more public attention than Tempora, probably because of the great sophistication and extent of the NSA's capacity to monitor and analyze raw data continuously acquired through cable traffic eavesdropping.[216]

As advanced as the monitoring and analysis may be, the tapping itself is, in principle, little different from "wiretapping" a pre-digital telephone line. In 2005 an Associated Press report published in *The New York Times* described a new nuclear submarine, the USS *Jimmy Carter* (SSN-23), which was equipped with "a special capability … to tap undersea cables," presumably by deploying Navy SEALs or other specialized divers to "physically place … tap[s] … along the [cable] route."[217] It was believed that these would be installed at "regeneration points" along the cable, connection to amplifiers that boost the strength of waning signals on their long journey. "At these spots, the fiber optics can be more easily tapped, because they are no longer bundled together, rather laid out individually."[218]

Let's acknowledge that performing a wiretap underwater is more difficult than shinnying up a telephone pole with some wire and alligator clips. Fortunately for tappers, portions of the trans-oceanic backbone are accessible on dry land—wherever the undersea cable makes landfall. Such tapping operations can be risky or even impossible on hostile coasts, but, lucky for the NSA and GCHQ, the location of the British Isles, a friendly country, makes it the terminus of many trans-Atlantic cable crossings. At these points, it is possible to insert optical "intercept probes," which "capture the light being sent across the [fiber optic] cable." Each "probe bounces the light through a prism, makes a copy of it, and turns it into binary data without disrupting the flow of the original Internet traffic."[219]

The technological infrastructure: what we must do

Technological infrastructure is a highly technical, complex, and, as pointed out, fluid subject. What is obvious and established, however, is that the physical components of the Internet are under the control of governments and corporations. They are therefore subject to government and corporate actions that may interfere with the free flow of information by monitoring, blocking, filtering, or intercepting it. Infrastructure components are also vulnerable to damage and destruction, both accidental and deliberate. Because their ownership and control is not uniformly regulated and often fragmentary, the vulnerability of the physical digital infrastructure is compounded even as accountability for adequate stewardship and security is diminished.

Diplomacy is inherently difficult. To the degree that it must depend on a fragmented, fragile, and insecure technological infrastructure, *cyberdiplomacy* is nearly impossible to conduct with any degree of confidence. We must generally harden both the physical and software components of the technological infrastructure of the Internet. This must be done on three levels:

1. **International:** While creating a practical international convention of cybersecurity is fraught with political difficulties (chapter 5), crafting international standards and best practices for the physical security of the global communications network should be far more feasible. The standards should be technical and specific, avoiding the ideological, moral, and political aspects of networking for interactive communications.
2. **National:** In coordination with international discussions,

governments should improve and harden their own communication infrastructures in the interests of national security. An important part of any national program must be an inventory and mapping of national cyber resources. Even the most complex of digital networks are, at one level, comparable to a chain made of links. The well-worn cliché about a chain being only as strong as its weakest link is well-worn for a reason. It is true. No nation can call itself secure without a secure digital infrastructure. No digital infrastructure can be secure without a thorough knowledge of its structure and individual components. Hidden vulnerabilities are the most dangerous.

3. **Local:** A chain is only as strong as its weakest link. Corporations, local government administrations, private-sector organizations, institutions, and each of us individually must take responsibility for making our own computers and local networks secure. Every node on the Internet is a point of opportunity and vulnerability. Internet security starts with each of us.

Legal infrastructures

The technology of the Internet runs counter to traditional political definitions of national sovereignty. For this reason, many early Internet theorists predicted that the global network spelled the end of nationhood since the Internet itself would become a kind of transnational super state. This has not happened, and it is almost certainly never going to happen. Nevertheless, many—but far from all—of the world's nation-states have struggled to craft international conventions to govern Internet technology, despite its essentially ungovernable nature as a technology that respects no national sovereignty. In chapter 5, we briefly reviewed, based on the disappointing performance of the existing cybercrime convention, the difficulties that lie in any attempt to craft an acceptable international cybersecurity convention.

The inadequacy, perhaps even failure, of the cybercrime convention should not relieve us of the responsibility of attempting to establish international standards for cybersecurity, which would create a more hospitable environment for building and conducting cyberdiplomacy. As suggested above, we can most feasibly begin by hammering out standards and best practices for the physical security of the global Internet. Beyond this, the international community should undertake the following steps:

1. Inventory, compile, evaluate, and work to reconcile all existing Internet and Internet-related legislation and regulations. The international community needs to assess the current state of law regarding the cross-border Internet, and it may be useful to build on that existing law.
2. Work toward consensus on common definitions. Simplify and clarify the context in which international agreements on cyber matters, including security, will be made by finding consensus on definitions of the basic terms of cyber law and cyberdiplomacy.
3. Work toward consensus on individual laws and regulations. Instead of endeavoring to create a single comprehensive grand convention on cybersecurity, work from a list of proposed international regulations. Proceed one at a time. Develop and act on those upon which there is majority agreement. Table anything on which there is majority dispute.
4. As soon as progress deemed sufficient has been made in 1, 2, and 3, begin work on a comprehensive cybersecurity convention.

On the national level, I believe that the United States should address issues relating to diplomacy in our digitally connected world by vigorously responding to specific events that call for cyberdiplomatic action. This follows the principle of American government set by Chief Justice John Marshall in *Marbury v. Madison* (5 U.S. 137; 1803), in which the high court's decision on a specific case established the precedent of judicial review under Article III of the U.S. Constitution. The precedent defined the leading function of the U.S. Supreme Court and therefore of the judicial branch of government.

As 2017 comes to a close at this writing, the single most visible crisis in cyberdiplomacy remains the interference in the U.S. presidential elections via network hacking by the government and/or leadership of the Russian Federation. The implications of this cyber "invasion," as some have characterized it, are profound. First, it is a possibly unprecedented (or at least never previously detected or revealed) use of the global Internet in an effort by a foreign power to influence and determine a public action that is central to U.S. government, U.S. democracy, and U.S. sovereignty. Second, it is an action that calls into question the legitimacy of the incoming administration.

Understandably, from partisan as well as non-partisan motives, some object to investigation of the Democratic National Committee hacks and related cyber intrusions. Indeed, the result of such investigations may yield some inconvenient truths or worse. Yet, as the extravagantly fictional embodiment of District Attorney of Orleans Parish (Louisiana) Jim Garrison proclaims in director Oliver Stone's extravagantly fictional film concerning the assassination of President John F. Kennedy, *JFK* (1991), "Let justice be done, though the heavens fall." It is an English translation of a Latin phrase of uncertain origin, *Fiat justitia ruat caelum,*[220] and it expresses the belief that justice must be realized regardless of the consequences. Ever since *Marbury v. Madison,* the government of the United States has written law and decided legal precedent from specific cases. This concrete approach is likely to be the most effective heuristic we have in crafting the basis of a cyberdiplomacy.

Extra-national infrastructures

Whatever nations and the global community may establish by way of legislation, regulation, and norms governing cyberdiplomacy, we must recognize that the Internet is ultimately extra-national, by which I mean that it is *in some measure* always beyond, outside of, or beside full national control. Both Jesus Christ and Karl Marx are among those who sought either to circumvent or supersede nationalism by defining a brotherhood of man (in the case of Christ) or an affiliation of class (in the case of Marx). The Internet succeeds beyond what either of these men achieved. It has created the ultimate peer-to-peer communications medium, directly connecting people with people or with other entities, or entities with entities.

Mobile technology, chiefly via smartphones, has greatly extended the reach and multiplied the effect of peer-to-peer relationships fostered or created by the Internet.[221] A number of mobile-centric platforms in various stages of development or deployment by such organizations as funf (funf.org), SwiftRiver (swiftly.org), Ushahidi (ushahidi.com), and PAX (paxreports.org), among others, are intended to provide benefits to individual, regional, and even global welfare, wellbeing, and progress. These organizations have developed or are developing ways to harness mobile devices to capture, record, process, visualize, map, disseminate, and analyze big data, including, for example, social network posts, video and photo posts, cell signals and call detail records, geolocation data, and e-commerce data. For an individual, this may simply mean tracking diet, exercise, and personal health. For a region, this may mean learning to understand trends in local development to improve the life, health, and wealth of the community. For a nation, this technology may enable beneficial changes in government and administration. Ushahidi, for instance, began as a website to map reports of violence in Kenya after the elections of 2008. For the world, mobile-centric Big Data projects may provide (as PAX aspires to create) "a global digital system to give early warning of wars and genocide." And for providers of e-commerce, the new mobile-centric Big Data technology may identify new markets while simultaneously providing the precise guidance needed to serve those markets efficiently and profitably.

The Jasmine Revolution in Tunisia (discussed in chapter 2) is an example of how mobile technology can simply vault over or cut out not only established governments but also traditional diplomacy to create national and diplomatic change via direct extra-national peer-to-peer action. Organizations and NGOs are already using mobile technology and Big Data analysis to drive social change with or without the cooperation of governments and sometimes despite governments. All nations must recognize the existence of extra-national infrastructures that are implementing peer-to-peer diplomacy and other forms of peer-to-peer activism. Governments fail to acknowledge these at their peril.

World enough and time

Digital technology has accelerated everything we see, do, or even think about. Whatever else cyberdiplomacy will be, it will be fast. In the meantime, it is likely that the official, formal deliberations of nations as well as international bodies will continue to lag behind digitally driven change for a long time.

We need viable national policies and international conventions and norms governing cyberdiplomacy and the associated area of cybersecurity. But we will not get these anytime soon. "Had we but world enough, and time," the seventeenth-century English poet Andrew Marvell argued in a poem to his "coy" mistress, "This coyness, Lady, were no crime ... / But at my back I always hear / Time's winged chariot hurrying near ..."[222]

We need policies and conventions, but the hacks of 2016-2017 alone,[223] including state-authorized attacks in violation of national sovereignty, have been so numerous and massive in scope and profound in implication that we clearly have neither world enough nor time to wait for our institutions and political leaders to get themselves up to the speed of digital transformation. We live in a political, economic, and diplomatic environment that presents an urgency beyond deliberation.

As suggested earlier in this chapter, corporations and other organizations, including local governments, as well as each of us as individuals, must urgently do all we can to secure our networks. This protects not only our own interests, but makes the Internet more resilient and therefore benefits our nation as well as our partners in whatever our endeavors may be. Cyber breaches cost \$400-\$500 billion in 2015, and costs are projected to reach \$2.1 trillion by 2019.[224]

This is staggering. But how do we even begin to calculate the cost of a state actor intervening via the Internet in the most basic function of the American democracy? Whatever the "cost," it is more than we can afford. There is great need for cyberdiplomacy, but no possibility of cyberdiplomacy without cybersecurity and universally accepted norms that both define and mandate cybersecurity. Without these, any attempt to build cyberdiplomacy is as doomed as the house of the foolish builder in the New Testament, who chose a foundation of sand instead of rock.[225] I propose that we emulate the peer-to-peer cyberdiplomacy of NGOs, activist organizations, and even contemporary revolutionaries.[226] We the people are the foundation rock we need.

On November 14, 2012, Senate Republicans blocked passage of the comprehensive Cybersecurity Act of 2012, objecting to what they deemed onerous government regulation of business.[227] This failure prompted President Barack Obama to issue, on February 12, 2013, an "Executive Order—Improving Critical Infrastructure Cybersecurity,"[228] which, contrary to the analyses of numerous critics,[229] took a welcome if tentative step or two toward bringing digitally interconnected private sector infrastructure under the defensive umbrellas of both the Department of Defense (DoD) and the Department of Homeland Security (DHS). Prior to the issuance of the Executive Order, the DoD assumed responsibility for the security of the nation's military cyber assets, and the DHS was charged with protecting civilian government cyber systems. Cyberattacks, of course, are made not only against the military and the civilian government, but also against the cyber assets, systems, and networks of the private sector. In fact, the private sector, which encompasses most of the American infrastructure and economy and is therefore the richest target of all, is the one most often in the crosshairs and most acutely at risk, yet is directly protected by neither the DoD nor the DHS.

President Obama's executive order was both a gesture toward government-regulated private sector security and a predicate for it. The order called for the creation of a preliminary "Cybersecurity Framework" and required "Agencies with responsibility for regulating the security of critical infrastructure [to] engage in a consultative process with DHS, OMB, and the National Security Staff to review the [document] … and determine if current cybersecurity regulatory requirements are sufficient given current and projected risks." Each agency was obliged to report on whether or not it "has clear authority to establish requirements based upon the Cybersecurity Framework to sufficiently address current and projected cyber risks to critical infrastructure, the existing authorities identified, and any additional authority required."[230] The predicate for something more than voluntary compliance with nationally mandated security standards for the private cyber sector is implied in the concluding five words of that final sentence, words that seem to invite government agencies to request whatever authority they need to "sufficiently address . . . cyber risks to critical infrastructure."

Defended neither by the DoD nor the DHS prior to the issuance of the Executive Order, private sector cyber was exposed and vulnerable. Did American business and industry therefore welcome the promise of the government's warm embrace? Hardly. Industry and business, including those enterprises responsible for critical infrastructure—the cyber-connected power grid, oil and gas pipeline systems, communications networks, and financial systems—have responded as they habitually do, by spurning "government regulation," and thus have perpetuated complicity in their vulnerability.

Somewhat surprisingly, President Trump renewed Obama's executive order. Whether effective legislation will replace it and make its provision permanent remains to be seen. The GOP is not friendly to statutory regulation, but, as of the close of 2017, it is anybody's guess as to whether the Republicans will hold their congressional majorities. For the immediate future at least, we will be left, then, to defend ourselves.

And that may be all right. For self-reliance is a posture Americans have assumed many times before. Its necessity is even contemplated in the Bill of Rights. The Second Amendment consists of a single sentence made up of two clauses separated by a comma: "A well regulated militia being necessary to the security of a free state, the right of the people to keep and bear arms shall not be infringed." In the context of the legal struggle between "gun control" proponents and "gun rights" advocates, the relationship between the clauses was sometimes a critical legal issue until the U.S. Supreme Court, in *District of Columbia v. Heller*, 554 U.S. 570 (2008), struck down the gun control party's contention that the first clause limits the second. The court held that, while the "prefatory clause" does announce a purpose—the maintenance of a "well regulated militia"—this purpose neither limits nor expands the scope of the "operative clause," which (the court affirmed) connotes an "individual right" to keep and bear arms.[231]

If *District of Columbia v. Heller* upholds "gun rights" in the operative clause, it does not entirely diminish the significance of the prefatory clause, which remains the Constitutional enshrinement of the militia concept. In the name of politics and ideology, the militiamen at

Lexington and Concord took a stand against the army of the British Empire, which refused to address their grievances. They took this stand by fighting a "kinetic" battle, a battle not of ideas, but of kinetic arms. In this sense, the operative clause, though still very much "operative" today, may be seen as a holdover from a world in which warfare was exclusively a matter of gunfire. The prefatory clause, even though it embodies the anachronistic-sounding word *militia* and the apparently antiquated concept it represents, is still capable of adaptation to our world, a world in which warfare may be fought by *kinetic* means or *cyber* means or some combination of the two. That is, while people and politicians passionately argue over second-clause Second Amendment gun rights, the largely neglected first-clause militia material is by far more constitutionally relevant to the cyberwarfare of today and tomorrow. It is about creating, under the national aegis, a body of individuals united in protecting their interests as citizens of the nation and the world. The Second Amendment was never about arming people against one another (or, even less, for the purpose of someday overthrowing the government they had together built), but for the purpose of uniting them in the common defense. The framers of the Constitution and its amendments were creating a nation. While that Constitution and those amendments to it, especially the Bill of Rights, certainly protect the rights of individuals, they assume that the nation is, first and foremost, a community. Call it, if you like, a network.

Not many years ago, the sentence *We are all connected* was a spiritual, theological, or metaphysical declaration. Today, it is a simple statement of fact. We *are* all connected—literally, by wires, optic fibers, and radio signals. It is also literally true that, against the networks and the nodes of these connections, there *are* attacks—daily, hourly, and by the hundreds of thousands. The remarkable growth of global digital technology has outstripped the ability of our national and global political leaders and deliberative bodies to create a new diplomacy suited to intensive, pervasive, and virtually universal connectivity. If we are to continue to benefit from the Internet instead of repeatedly falling victim to it, we must, as a people, redefine *government, military, private sector enterprise*, and the *individual* as members of a single *community* empowered to provide for the "common defense." This will require an intelligent and selective embrace of government regulation and a significant intellectual, political, and cultural shift in the prevailing concepts of individual privacy, nationhood, international relations, and diplomacy. Yet, despite the daunting prospect of embarking on a journey of radical rethinking, neither the embrace nor the shift required is entirely novel. Both were contemplated well over two centuries ago by the framers of the Constitution and, again, at the turn of the twentieth century, by lawmakers who sought to define, expand, and implement a key provision of that Constitution's Second Amendment in the Militia Act of 1903.[232]

Driven by the urgency of unprecedented technological innovation, I propose a national revaluation of values based on a *return* to values at the core of our nation's founding. The specific form of this revaluation is what we might call a "cybermilitia." The cybermilitia I envision is not an organization, military or paramilitary, but a state of mind, an attitude, an orientation, and a set of behaviors. Call it a social contract, if you like.

George Mason, one of the framers of the Constitution, posed the rhetorical question, "Who are the militia?" which he answered: "They consist now of the whole people, except for a few public officers."[233] We are, all of us, the cybermilitia, and we are facing an endless invasion that calls for perpetual defense. Our service required does not involve parades, KP, or rifle practice. For most of us, cybermilitia service is neither more nor less than an attitude about and an approach to the computing we do. Cybermilitia asks us to recognize a common obligation to enter a *militia state of mind* with respect to cybersecurity. It calls on us to accept government regulation for the purpose of "common defense" and a willingness to define—or redefine—"privacy" in the interests of "community." It further calls for recognition of the transnational and trans-sectorial nature of cyberspace. Membership in the cybermilitia entails recognizing the fall of barriers that have traditionally separated government, military, and private sectors. All sectors and every individual meet at multiple nodes in networked cyberspace, a domain that no more respects administrative boundaries than it does national borders.

In addition to these political and ideological requirements, cybermilitia members should, for reasons of their own individual security as well as for the common defense, educate themselves about the opportunities, challenges, and risks of living and working online. For these same reasons, they should enthusiastically practice safe computing to protect their valuable data and the data others (including employers, employees, merchants, and clients) entrust to them. They should become well versed in matters of cybersecurity and safe computing.

Most of us are members of what 10 U.S. Code § 246 – Militia: composition and classes calls the "unorganized militia." We are not an organized body of defenders, so much as holders of *militia state of mind* a thoroughly informed willingness to accept and comply with certain directions and regulations in the interests of collective security. But there is also an "organized militia," which was formally defined by the Militia

Act of 1903 (and updated by 10 U.S. Code § 246), based on the Second Amendment.[234] As applied to the cybermilitia concept, the organized militia may be thought of as consisting of two segments.

The first segment includes those leaders of the IT and security industries who are willing to create and share best security and privacy practices not only on a B2B basis, but with the broader consumer public. Call this, if you like, open-source cyber defense. Many in the industry have already stepped up with educational programs and low-cost, free, or freemium security products for the consumer market. Such programs and products are not only the elements of good corporate citizenship, they have become, in our hyperconnected age, essential to good citizenship, period. They are the elements of survival and prosperity in a wired civilization, where so much of the economy lives online.

The second component of the "organized" cybermilitia is composed of public-spirited professionals, academics, and stakeholders in IT, digital technology, and Internet industries, as well as technology and policy bloggers and journalists. Motivated people in these categories may be uncomfortable thinking of themselves as units in *any* kind of militia, even a cybermilitia. Fortunately for them, there is no absolute need to adopt the term. In fact, a more appropriate descriptor may be found in a coinage by Alexander Klimburg of the International Cyber Center at George Mason University. He calls these groups "Security Trust Networks" (STNs). As Klimburg defines them, STNs are groups that study and advise on aspects of cybersecurity, operating independently of any agency of government or private sector. Even when the state or a corporate entity commissions or convenes a particular STN, makes use of the expertise and advice it offers, and perhaps provides all or some funding and other support, it exerts minimal control over the group. The effectiveness of an STN is in its independence and its insistence on being defined by trust and ethics rather than by allegiance to policy or profit. Operating within the law, "its members share a common moral code . . . based on 'doing the right thing.' The shared moral mission of the STN is its official *raison d'être*." And the fact is that the U.S. government and governments of other Western nations already turn to STNs for technical expertise and advice on cyber matters.[235]

A prime example of an STN is the "open source intelligence (OSINT) experiment" Jeffrey Carr launched on August 22, 2008. Called Project Grey Goose, it was an independent attempt to investigate the origin and structure of the attacks that were being launched on Georgian government websites during the five-day Russo-Georgian War (2008). Carr's STN was able to demonstrate that these attacks, which "gave the appearance of being entirely spontaneous, an act of support by Russian 'hacktivists' who were not part of the RF [Russian Federation] military," were in fact very closely tied to the Russian government and to "RF military actions dating back to 2002."[236]

It is important to understand that the Militia Act of 1903 and the additional legislation that followed it *created* no militia. Instead, it *recognized the existence* of one—the militia alluded to in the Second Amendment—and merely defined and implemented it. I suggest that we enact a similar recognition among the nation's Internet stakeholders. If the nation chooses to build on its Constitution, laws, and traditions to recognize citizens as members of the cybermilitia, then the roles and obligations of government (both military and civil), the corporate private sector, and individual Internet users must be clearly defined by law.

What would that law look like? The Internet has reached a level of technical, intellectual, and economic sophistication that enables it to serve as a platform to convey and enhance the values of those who use it. We see the cybermilitia as an expression of American values, which derive from a revolutionary tradition that is both older and more sustainable than its revolutionary counterparts in Russia and China. American values simultaneously promote individual and collective rights, both individual human rights and the commonweal. Whatever laws and regulations we may create for the Internet must mandate strategies and technologies to maintain the revolutionary simultaneity of both self and nation. Certainly, any regulations must avoid "Big Brother" aspects of government control in establishing and enforcing online security standards. Instead, they must promote, not compel, compliance at all levels. A government that requires the presence and service of a cybermilitia must treat the private sector (both corporate and individual) as a *free* militia, not as a conscripted army or a subject population.

For the individual Internet stakeholder, the emphasis should be on education to promote secure computing that benefits all stakeholders. Incentive rather than coercion should be the instrument of motivation. As part of its investment in hardening the backbone and other infrastructures of the Internet, the government may subsidize the development of technologies that promote control and ownership of individual personal data by the individual person who creates that data. To the degree that individual users are given a full ownership stake in the Internet, they will have a greater motive to defend that collective national asset.

For private sector enterprise, government "regulation" should be delivered as an enabling service, not a restricting demand. It should clearly promote the general welfare and provide for the common defense, creating the conditions in which commerce can survive and thrive.

Regulation should not merely "relate to" infrastructure, it should become an essential aspect of infrastructure, the shared security on which citizens and their enterprises can rely. In this way, the infrastructures of our interconnected world become the equivalent of sovereign territory—not exclusive, but sovereign nonetheless—and therefore provides both a platform and a rationale from which to conduct credible, enforceable cyberdiplomacy with other nations and people.

ABOUT THE AUTHOR

Siobhan MacDermott leads the Global Cyber Public Policy team of Bank of America and is responsible for the bank's participation in programs dedicated to improving cyber resiliency of the global financial system.

Ms. MacDermott was Risk and Cybersecurity Principal at EY (formerly Ernst & Young), consulting to Fortune 500 boards on cyber. Before this, she was the Chief Information Security Officer for Utilidata, Inc. and Chief Policy Officer for AVG Technologies. She has been instrumental in directing strategy, government relations, global policy, and executive communications for numerous financial services and technical companies across the globe.

Vice Chair of the Fund for Peace and Associate Fellow for the Global Fellowship Initiative for the Geneva Centre for Security Policy in Switzerland, Ms. MacDermott is a Senior Fellow of the Edward R. Murrow Center for a Digital World at the Fletcher School of Law and Diplomacy at Tufts University and serves as a Board Member for the Center for Global Risk and Security at the Rand Corporation. She graduated from Temple University with a Bachelor of Arts in German Language and Literature. She holds a Master of Business Administration from Thunderbird School of Global Management and a Global Master of Arts in Law and Diplomacy
from the Fletcher School at Tufts University. She has worked in eight countries and speaks five languages. The Folded Paper is her sixth book.

Notes

Preface

[1] U.S. Census Bureau News (November 17, 2017),
https://www.census.gov/retail/mrts/www/data/pdf/ec_current.pdf.
[2] J. J. Colao, "Five Trends Driving Traditional Retail Towards Extinction,"
Forbes (December 13, 2012),
http://www.forbes.com/sites/jjcolao/2012/12/13/five-trends-driving-traditional-retail-towards-extinction/#4690ab7578bc.
[3] Dave Gilreath, "Online shopping hasn't killed brick-and-mortar retailers,"
ABC News (October 12, 2017), http://abcnews.go.com/Business/online-shopping-killed-brick-mortar-retailers/story?id=50367943.
[4] Daniel Newman. "Top 6 Digital Transformation Trends in Government,"
Forbes (June 29, 2017),
https://www.forbes.com/sites/danielnewman/2017/06/29/top-6-digital-transformation-trends-in-government/#1f48d5f27efc.
[5] Information relating to this phenomenon is far too abundant to cite. The best place to begin to explore "Russian meddling" is with the remarkable Wikipedia article, "Russian interference in the 2016 United States elections,"
https://en.wikipedia.org/wiki/Russian_interference_in_the_2016_United_States_elections.

Introduction

[6] For this translation and a discussion of the definition, see Thomas Waldman, "Politics and War: Clausewitz's Paradoxical Equaiton," *Parameters* (Autumn 2010), 1-13,
http://strategicstudiesinstitute.army.mil/pubs/parameters/articles/2010autumn/waldman.pdf.
[7] For an account of the 2007 attack on Estonia, see Jeffrey Carr, *Inside Cyber Warfare.* (N.p.: O'Reilly Media, 2011), Kindle Edition, chap. 7;
[8] Timothy Stenovec, "Shell Arctic Ready Hoax Website By Greenpeace Takes Internet By Storm," *The Huffington Post* (July 19, 2012),
http://www.huffingtonpost.com/2012/07/18/shell-arctic-ready-hoax-greenpeace_n_1684222.html.
[9] Ryan Holiday, "How Greenpeace Manipulated the Media Like a Pro: Analyzing the Shell Oil Hoax," *Forbes* (June 15, 2012),
http://www.forbes.com/sites/ryanholiday/2012/06/15/how-greenpeace-manipulated-the-media-like-a-pro-analyzing-the-shell-oil-hoax/#43ddeee7ce18.
[10] Quoted in "Safeguard Your Reputation and Bottom Line with Corporate Diplomacy," *Wharton@Work* (January 2014),

http://executiveeducation.wharton.upenn.edu/thought-leadership/wharton-at-work/2014/01/corporate-diplomacy.

[11] Max Seddon, "Documents Show How Russia's Troll Army Hit America," *BuzzFeed News* (June 2, 2014), https://www.buzzfeed.com/maxseddon/documents-show-how-russias-troll-army-hit-america?utm_term=.iynkDLojJ7#.aszXkYQ4yD, and Laura Sydell, "How Russian Propaganda Spreads on Social Media, *All Tech Considered* (October 29, 2017), https://www.npr.org/sections/alltechconsidered/2017/10/29/560461835/how-russian-propaganda-spreads-on-social-media.

Chapter 1

[12] Quoted in Christopher Hibbert, *The Virgin Queen: Elizabeth I, Genius of the Golden Age* (New York: Da Capo Press, 1991), 133.

[13] Thomas Jefferson to Edward Carrington, January 16, 1787, in Merrill D. Peterson, ed., *The Portable Thomas Jefferson* (New York: Penguin, 1976), 415.

[14] Thomas Jefferson to Thomas Cooper, November 29, 1802, *American History from Revolution to Reconstruction and Beyond*, *http://www.let.rug.nl/usa/presidents/thomas-jefferson/letters-of-thomas-jefferson/jefl148.php*.

[15] Thomas Jefferson to Marquis de Lafayette, November 4, 1823, *Founders Early Access*, http://rotunda.upress.virginia.edu/founders/default.xqy?keys=FOEA-print-04-02-02-3843.

[16] Thomas Jefferson to George Washington, June 1796, quoted in John P. Foley, ed., *The Jefferson Cyclopedia* (New York: Funk and Wagnalls, 1900), 640.

[17] Thomas Jefferson to James Madison, July 3, 1811, Thomas Jefferson, *The Works of Thomas Jefferson* (New York: Cosimo Classics, 2009), 12: 209.

[18] For a transcript, see "Fireside Chat 1: On the Banking Crisis (March 12, 1933), http://millercenter.org/president/fdroosevelt/speeches/speech-3298.

[19] Archibald MacLeish, "A Superstition Is Destroyed," December 2, 1941, quoted in Philip Seib, *Broadcasts from the Blitz: How Edward R. Murrow Helped Lead America Into War* (Washington, DC: Potomac Books, 2006), 148.

[20] Steven Casey, *Cautious Crusade: Franklin D. Roosevelt, American Public Opinion and the War against Nazi Germany* (New York: Oxford Universisty Press, 2001), 25-29.

[21] Philip Seib, *Real-Time Diplomacy: Politics and Power in the Social Media Era* (New York: Palgrave Macmillan, 2012), Kindle ed., chapter 3.

[22] Seib, Kindle ed., chapter 3.

[23] Seib, Kindle ed., chapter 3.

24 "Death Strip: Berlin Pays Tribute to Last Person Shot Crossing Wall," *Spiegel Online* (February 6, 2009), http://www.spiegel.de/international/germany/death-strip-berlin-pays-tribute-to-last-person-shot-crossing-wall-a-605967.html.
25 Seib, Kindle ed., chapter 3.
26 See Alan Axelrod, "The Television War," in *Political History of America's Wars* (Washington, DC: CQ Press, 2007), 435-436.
27 See Alan Axelrod, "The Tet Crisis (1968), in *Political History of America's Wars* (Washington, DC: CQ Press, 2007), 436.
28 Robert Wiener, *Live from Baghdad* (New York: Doubleday, 1992), 253.
29 Lawrence Grossman, "How to Improve TV Network News: A Plan for the Next War,"*Nieman Reports* (Summer 1991), 27, http://1e9svy22oh333mryr83l4s02.wpengine.netdna-cdn.com/wp-content/uploads/2014/04/Summer-1991_150.pdf.
30 Seib, Kindle ed., chapter 3.
31 Seib, Kindle ed., chapter 3.
32 George F. Kennan, *At a Century's Ending: Reflections, 1982-1995* (New York: W. W. Norton, 1996), 297.
33 Chris Taylor, "Smartphone Sales Overtake PCs for the First Time," Mashable (February 3. 2012), http://mashable.com/2012/02/03/smartphone-sales-overtake-pcs/#z6bW03RKr8qE.
34 James O'Toole, "Mobile apps overtake PC Internet usage in U.S.," CNNTech (February 28, 2014), http://money.cnn.com/2014/02/28/technology/mobile/mobile-apps-internet/.
35 Peter Lucas, Joe Ballay, Mickey McManus, *Trillions: Thriving in the Emerging Information Ecology* (Hoboken, NJ: John Wiley, 2012), 9.
36 Larry Diamond, "Liberation Technology," *Journal of Democracy* 21, no. 3 (July 2010), 70, http://isites.harvard.edu/fs/docs/icb.topic980025.files/Wk%2011_Nov%2011th/Diamond_2010_Liberation%20Technologies.pdf.
37 Diamond, 70.
38 Sophie Beach, "Rise of Rights?" *China Digital Times* (May 27, 2005), http://chinadigitaltimes.net/2005/05/rise-of-rights/.
39 Diamond, 69.
40 Diamond, 70.
41 Marlo Machado, "The Revolution Will Be Tweeted," *The World Post* (July 3, 2013; updated September 23, 2013), http://www.huffingtonpost.com/mario-machado/the-revolution-will-be-tw_1_b_3530075.html.

Chapter 2

42 Ninoy Aquino, "Worth Dying For," https://www.youtube.com/watch?v=zuEPFt-Dd-Q.

---

[43] Transparency International. *Global Corruption Report* (2004), 13, http://www.transparency.org/content/download/4459/26786/file/Introduction_to _political_corruption.pdf.

[44] Howard Rheingold, *Smart Mobs: The Next Social Revolution* (New York: Basic Books, 2003), 158.

[45] Philip Seib, *Real-Time Diplomacy: Politics and Power in the Social Media Era* (New York: Palgrave Macmillan, 2012), Kindle ed., chapter 6.

[46] Manuel Castells, Mireia Fernandez-Ardevol, Jack Linchuan Qiu, and Araba Sey, "Electronic Communication and Socio-Political Mobilisation: A New Form of Civil Society," in Marlies Glasius, Mary Kaldor, and Helmut Anheir, eds., *Global Civil Society* (London: Sage, 2006), 112-114.

[47] Larry Diamond, "Liberation Technology," *Journal of Democracy* 21, no. 3 (July 2010), 69-83.

[48] Seib, Kindle ed. chapter 6.

[49] Malcolm Gladwell, "Does Egypt Need Twitter?" *The New Yorker* (February 2, 2011), http://www.newyorker.com/news/news-desk/does-egypt-need-twitter.

[50] Colin Delany, "How Social Media Accelerated Tunisia's Revolution: An Inside View, eopolitics.com (February 10, 2011), http://www.epolitics.com/2011/02/10/how-social-media-accelerated-tunisias-revolution-an-inside-view/. The article discusses Andy Carvin, *Distant Witness: Social Media, the Arab Spring, and a Journalism Revolution* (New York: CUNY Journalism Press, 2012), at the time forthcoming.

[51] Clay Shirky, "The Political Power of Social Media," *Foreign Affairs* 90, no. 1 (January/February 2011), 29.

[52] Charlie Beckett, "After Tunisia and Egypt: Towards a New Typology of Media and Networked Political Change, *Polis: Jounrlaism and Society at the LSE,* http://blogs.lse.ac.uk/polis/2011/02/11/after-tunisia-and-egypt-towards-a-new-typology-of-media-and-networked-political-change/.

[53] Seib, chapter 6.

[54] Paul Goodman, *Communitas: Means of Livelihood and Ways of Life* (Chicago: University of Chicago Press, 1947).

[55] John Perry Barlow, "A Declaration of the Independence of Cyberspace," https://projects.eff.org/~barlow/Declaration-Final.html.

[56] Both Negroponte and Krugman quoted in Jack Goldsmith and Tim Wu, *Who Controls the Internet: Illusions of a Borderless World* (New York: Oxford University Press, 2006), 4.

[57] Volodymyr V. Lysenko and Kevin C. Desouza, "Role of Internet-based information flows and technologies in electoral revolutions: The case of Ukraine's Orange Revolution," *First Monday: Peer-Reviewed Journal of the Internet* (vol. 15, no. 9, September 6, 2010), http://firstmonday.org/ojs/index.php/fm/article/view/2992/2599.

[58] Joshua Goldstein, "The Role of Digital Networked Technologies in the Ukrainian Orange Revolution," Internet and Democracy Case Study Series (December 2007),

http://cyber.law.harvard.edu/sites/cyber.law.harvard.edu/files/Goldstein_Ukrain e_2007.pdf, 9.

[59] Seib, chapter 7.

[60] Aaron Smith and Lee Rainie, "The Internet and the 2008 Election" (Pew Internet and American Life Project, June 15, 2008), http://www.pewinternet.org/files/old-media/Files/Reports/2008/PIP_2008_election.pdf.pdf.

[61] Matthew Fraser and Soumitra Dutta, "Barack Obama and the Facebook Election," *U.S. News and World Report* (November 19, 2008), http://www.usnews.com/opinion/articles/2008/11/19/barack-obama-and-the-facebook-election.

[62] Ask Factcheck, "Advertising Money: McCain vs. Obama" (November 3, 2008), http://www.factcheck.org/2008/11/advertising-money-mccain-vs-obama/.

[63] Seib, chapter 6.

[64] Bill Allison, Mira Rojanasakul, Brittany Harris, and Cedric Sam, "Tracking the 2016 Presidential Money Race," *Bloomberg Politics* (December 9, 2016), https://www.bloomberg.com/politics/graphics/2016-presidential-campaign-fundraising; Associated Press, "The candidate ad spending race" (updated November 15, 2016), http://elections.ap.org/content/ad-spending; Dana Milbank, "Trump's fake-news presidency," *Washington Post* (November 18, 2016), https://www.washingtonpost.com/opinions/trumps-fake-news-presidency/2016/11/18/72cc7b14-ad96-11e6-977a-1030f822fc35_story.html?utm_term=.203e71cb7b64.

[65] Seib, chapter 6.

[66] Seib, chapter 6.

[67] See, for example, Katie Worth, "Lone Wolf Attacks Are Becoming More Common—And More Deadly," *Frontline* (July 14, 2016), http://www.pbs.org/wgbh/frontline/article/lone-wolf-attacks-are-becoming-more-common-and-more-deadly/, and Margaret Coker, Eric Schmitt, and Rukmini Callimachi, "With Loss of its Caliphate, ISIS May Return to Guerilla Roots," *New York Times* (October 18, 2017), https://www.nytimes.com/2017/10/18/world/middleeast/islamic-state-territory-attacks.html?_r=0.

[68] David Saranga, "The Use of New Media in Public Diplomacy," *One Jerusalem* (June 3, 2009), http://onej.org/analysis/1209-7the-use-of-new-media-in-public-diplomacy.

[69] Israel in New York, tweet posted December 29, 2008, https://twitter.com/IsraelinNewYork/status/1084375595.

[70] Seib, chapter 6.

[71] Seib, chapter 5.

[72] Ramy Raoof, "Mobile Tactics for Participants in Peaceful Assemblies, Global Voices Advocacy)May 26, 2011), http://advocacy.globalvoicesonline.org/2011/05/26/mobile-tactics-for-participants-in-peaceful-assemblies/.

73 Seib, chapter 5.
74 Seib, chapter 6.

Chapter 3

75 Andrew Sullivan, "The Revolution Will Be Twittered," *The Atlantic,* June 13, 2009, http://www.theatlantic.com/daily-dish/archive/2009/06/the-revolution-will-be-twittered/200478/.
76 Evgeny Morozov, *The Net Delusion: The Dark Side of Internet Freedom* (New York: Public Affairs, 2011), Kindle ed., Introduction.
77 Marc Ambinder, "The Revolution Will Be Twittered," *The Atlantic,* June 15, 2009,http://www.theatlantic.com/politics/archive/2009/06/the-revolution-will-be-twittered/19376/.
78 Ross Kaminsky, "Iran's Twitter Revolution," *Human Events,* June 18, 2009, http://humanevents.com/2009/06/18/irans-twitter-revolution/.
79 Both quoted in Morozov, Kindle ed., Introduction.
80 Clay Shirky, "How social media can make history," TED, June 2009, http://www.ted.com/talks/clay_shirky_how_cellphones_twitter_facebook_can_make_history?language=en.
81 Mark Pfeifle, "A Nobel Peace Prize for Twitter," *The Shristian Science Monitor,* July 6, 2009, http://www.csmonitor.com/Commentary/Opinion/2009/0706/p09s02-coop.html.
82 Brown quoted in Morozov, Kindle ed., chapter 1.
83 Morozov, Kindle ed., Introduction.
84 Dwight D. Eisenhower, "Address Before the General Assembly of the United Nations on Peaceful Uses of Atmomic Energy, New York City," December 8, 1953, http://www.presidency.ucsb.edu/ws/?pid=9774.
85 Morozov, Kindle ed., chapter 1.
86 Brad Stone and Noam Cohen, "Social Networks Spread Defiance Online," *The New York Times,* June 15, 2009, http://www.nytimes.com/2009/06/16/world/middleeast/16media.html?_r=0.
87 Morozov, Kindle ed., chapter 1.
88 Morozov, Kindle ed., chapter 1.
89 Mark Evans, "A Look at Twitter in Iran," Sysmos blog, June 21, 2009, http://blog.sysomos.com/2009/06/21/a-look-at-twitter-in-iran/.
90 "Moeed Ahmad on the Problems with Twitter," *Big Ideas,* March 2, 2010, http://www.abc.net.au/tv/bigideas/stories/2010/03/02/2829652.htm.
91 All quoted in Morozov, Kindle ed., chapter 1.
92 Golnaz Esfandiari, "The Twitter Devolution," *Foreign Policy,* June 8, 2010, http://foreignpolicy.com/2010/06/08/the-twitter-devolution/.
93 Morozov, Kindle ed., chapter 1.
94 Reza Zia-Ebrahimi, "Bombard Iran … with Broadband, *The Guardian,* February 24, 2010,

http://www.theguardian.com/commentisfree/2010/feb/24/iran-protest-internet-satellite.

[95] Carla Marshall, "Cat Videos on YouTube: 2 Million Uploads, 25 Billion Views," *ReelSeo: The Video Marketer's Guide,* October 29, 2014, http://www.reelseo.com/2-million-cat-videos-youtube/.

[96] Hillary Rodham Clinton, "Remarks on Internet Freedom," The Newseum, January 21, 2010, http://www.state.gov/secretary/20092013clinton/rm/2010/01/135519.htm.

[97] Clinton, http://www.state.gov/secretary/20092013clinton/rm/2010/01/135519.htm.

[98] Morozov, Kindle ed., chapter 2.

[99] Newton N. Minow, "Television and the Public Interest," delivered May 9, 1961, National Association of Broadcasters, Washington, DC, http://www.americanrhetoric.com/speeches/newtonminow.htm.

[100] Clinton, http://www.state.gov/secretary/20092013clinton/rm/2010/01/135519.htm.

[101] Thomas L. Friedman, *The Lexus and the Olive Tree: Understanding Globalization* (New York: Random House, 2000), 70.

[102] Benito Mussolini, *My Rise and Fall* (reprints *My Autobiography* [1928] and *History of a Year* [1945]; New York: Da Capo, 1998), 3.

[103] John Perry Barlow, "A Declaration of the Independence of Cyberspace," https://projects.eff.org/~barlow/Declaration-Final.html.

[104] Negroponte quoted in Jack Goldsmith and Tim Wu, *Who Controls the Internet: Illusions of a Borderless World,* New York: Oxford University Press, 2006), 4.

[105] Larry Diamond, "Liberation Technology," *Journal of Democracy*, vol. 21, no. 3 (Jukly 2010), 69, http://isites.harvard.edu/fs/docs/icb.topic980025.files/Wk%2011_Nov%2011th/Diamond_2010_Liberation%20Technologies.pdf.

[106] William J. Dobson, "Computer Programmer Takes on the World's Despots," *Newsweek,* August 6, 2010, http://www.newsweek.com/computer-programmer-takes-worlds-despots-71587.

[107] "Innovator of the Year, Winner, Austin Heap," *The Guardian,* March 26, 2010, http://www.theguardian.com/megas/winner-2010-innovator-year-austin-heap.

[108] Cecilia Kang, "Haystack stops tests of Iran anti-censor software amid security concerns," *The Washington Post,* September 13, 2010, http://voices.washingtonpost.com/posttech/2010/09/haystack_stops_testing_its_ant.html?wprss=posttech.

[109] Simon Phipps, "Award-Winning Haystack Security System Could Risk Iranian Lives, *ComputerworldUK,* September 14, 2010, http://www.computerworlduk.com/blogs/simon-says/-awardwinning-haystack-security-system-could-risk-iranian-lives--3569566/.

[110] Diamond,

http://isites.harvard.edu/fs/docs/icb.topic980025.files/Wk%2011_Nov%2011th/
Diamond_2010_Liberation%20Technologies.pdf, 69.

[111] Diamond,
http://isites.harvard.edu/fs/docs/icb.topic980025.files/Wk%2011_Nov%2011th/
Diamond_2010_Liberation%20Technologies.pdf,_70.
[112] Clay Shirky, "The Political Power of Social Media," *Foreign Affairs* 90, no.
1 (January/February 2011), 29.
[113] Shirky.
[114] Charlie Beckett, "After Tunisia and Egypt: Towards a New Typology of
Media and Networked Political Change," *POLIS: Journalism and Society at the
LSE,* http://blogs.lse.ac.uk/polis/2011/02/11/after-tunisia-and-egypt-towards-a-
new-typology-of-media-and-networked-political-change/.
[115] Philip Seib, *Real-Time Diplomacy: Politics and Power in the Social Media
Era* (New York: Palgrave Macmillan, 2012), Kindle ed,, chapter 6.
[116] Jack Goldsmith and Tim Wu, *Who Controls the Internet? Illusions of a
Borderless World* (New York: Oxford University Press, 2006), Preface.
[117] Goldsmith and Wu, 7.
[118] Goldsmith and Wu, 29-46.

Chapter 4

[119] Evgeny Morozov, *The Net Delusion* (New York: PublicAffairs, 2011).
[120] Jack Goldsmith and Tim Wu, *Who Controls the Internet? Illusions of a
Borderless World* (New York: Oxford University Press, 2006).
[121] Morozov, 217.
[122] Morozov, 218.
[123] Morozov, 218.
[124] Morozov, 219.
[125] Harper Neidig, "Franken blasts Facebook for accepting rubles for U.S.
election ads," *The Hill* (October 31, 2017),
http://thehill.com/policy/technology/358102-franken-blasts-facebook-for-
accepting-rubles-for-us-election-ads.
[126] Morozov, 71.
[127] J. R. Smith and Siobhan MacDermott, *Wide Open Privacy: Strategies for the
Digital Life* (Birmingham, MI: IT-Harvest Press, 2012); Kindle ed., chapter 2.
[128] Julia Angwin, "The Web's New Gold Mine: Your Secrets," *The Wall Street
Journal* (July 30, 2010),
http://www.wsj.com/articles/SB10001424052748703940904575395073512989404.
[129] J. Yan, N. Liu, N., G. Wang, W, Zhang, J. Yun J., and Z. Chen, "How much
can behavioral targeting help online advertising?" *Proceedings of the 18
International Conference on World Wide Web* (Madrid, Spain 2009),ACM, 261-
270.

130 Jianqing Chen and Jan Stallaert, "Attention, Shoppers: Store Is Tracking Your Cell," *New York Times,* July 14, 2013, http://www.nytimes.com/2013/07/15/business/attention-shopper-stores-are-tracking-your-cell.html?pagewanted=all.*New York Times.*
131 Global Network Initiative website, https://www.globalnetworkinitiative.org/.
132 Morozov, 23.
133 Ewen MacAskill, "NSA paid millions to cover Prism compliance costs for tech companies," *The Guardian,* August 23, 2013, http://www.theguardian.com/world/2013/aug/23/nsa-prism-costs-tech-companies-paid.
134 Barton Gellman and Laura Poitras, "U.S., British intelligence mining data from nine U.S. Internet companies in broad secret program, *The Guardian,* June 7, 2013, http://www.washingtonpost.com/investigations/us-intelligence-mining-data-from-nine-us-internet-companies-in-broad-secret-program/2013/06/06/3a0c0da8-cebf-11e2-8845-d970ccb04497_story.html.
135 Dominic Rushe, "Yahoo $250,000 daily fine over NSA data refusal was set to double 'every week,'" *The Guardian,* September 12, 2014, http://www.theguardian.com/world/2014/sep/11/yahoo-nsa-lawsuit-documents-fine-user-data-refusal.
136 Byron Acohido, "Latest PRISM discolsures shouldn't worry consumers," *USA Today,* September 5, 2013, http://www.usatoday.com/story/cybertruth/2013/09/05/latest-prism-disclosures-shouldnt-worry-consumers/2773495/.
137 Chelsea Manning, "'I am Chelsea': Read Manning's full statement," *Today News,* August 22, 2013, http://www.today.com/news/i-am-chelsea-read-mannings-full-statement-6C10974052.
138 Evan Hansen, "Manning-Lamo Chat Logs Revealed, *Wired,* July 13, 2011, http://www.wired.com/2011/07/manning-lamo-logs/.
139 Hansen, http://www.wired.com/2011/07/manning-lamo-logs/.
140 "Open Secrets: WikiLeaks, War and American Diplomacy," *The New York Times,* [January 26, 2011], http://www.nytimes.com/projects/2011/video/opensecrets/.
141 Hansen, http://www.wired.com/2011/07/manning-lamo-logs/.
142 Woodrow Wilson, "President Woodrow Wilson;s 14 Points (1918), http://www.ourdocuments.gov/doc.php?flash=true&doc=62.
143 Michael Moore and Oliver Stone, "WikiLeaks and Free Speech," *The New York Times,* August 20, 2012, http://www.nytimes.com/2012/08/21/opinion/wikileaks-and-the-global-future-of-free-speech.html?_r=2&.
144 Zack Beauchamp, "The WikiLeaks-Russia connection started way before the 2016 election," Vox (January 6, 2017), https://www.vox.com/world/2017/1/6/14179240/wikileaks-russia-ties; David A. Graham, "The Astonishing Transformation of Julian Assange," *The Atlantic* (January 5, 2017),

https://www.theatlantic.com/politics/archive/2017/01/assange-man-in-the-news/512243/.

145 Jonathan Foreman, "The WikiLeaks War on America," *Commentary* (January 1, 2011), https://www.commentarymagazine.com/articles/the-wikileaks-war-on-america/.

146 Max Boot, "WikiLeaks Has Joined the Trump Administration," *Foreign Policy* (March 8, 2017), http://foreignpolicy.com/2017/03/08/wikileaks-has-joined-the-trump-administration/.

147 Office of the Director of National Intelligence, "2012 Report on Security Clearance Determinations," http://www.fas.org/sgp/othergov/intel/clear-2012.pdf.

148 Noam Scheiber, "Why'd He Do It? *New Republic,* June 10, 2013, http://www.newrepublic.com/article/113425/edward-snowden-nsa-spying-leak-motive.

149 Maya Rhodan, "Dick Cheney Calls Snowden a 'Traitor,' Defends NSA," *Time,* October 28, 2013, http://swampland.time.com/2013/10/28/dick-cheney-calls-snowden-a-traitor-defends-nsa/.

150 European Commission, *Proposal for a Regulation of the European Parliament and of the Council on the Protection of Individuals with Regard to the Processing of Personal Data and on the Free Movement of Such Data (General Data Protection Regulation),* January 25, 2012, http://ec.europa.eu/justice/data-protection/document/review2012/com_2012_11_en.pdf.

151 IAPP, "Will NSA Revelations Be a Game Changer?" http://view.iapp-email.com/?j=fec1157670660d7a&m=fe9413707564027a72&ls=fe581073736d0c7d7010&l=ff2c15777260&s=fe911c787466037e74&jb=ffcf14&ju=fe9411747561037c70&r=0.

152 James Risen and Nick Wingfield, "Web's Reach Binds N.S.A. and Silicon Valley Leaders," *The New York Times,* June 19, 2013, http://www.nytimes.com/2013/06/20/technology/silicon-valley-and-spy-agency-bound-by-strengthening-web.html?pagewanted=all&_r=1&.

153 Delegation of the European Union to the United States, "EU-U.S. Justice and Home Affairs Ministerial in Dublin—Speaking Points of Vice-President Reding and Commissioner Malmström," http://www.euintheus.org/press-media/eu-u-s-justice-and-home-affairs-ministerial-in-dublin-speaking-points-of-vice-president-reding-and-commissioner-malmstrom/.

154 Daily Dashboard, "After PRISM, EU Trust in U.S. Questioned," June 18, 2013, https://www.privacyassociation.org/news/a/after-prism-eu-trust-in-u.s.-questioned.

155 Barton Gellman and Jerry Markon, "Edward Snowden says motive behind leaks was to expose 'surveillance state,'" *The Washington Post,* June 10, 2013, http://www.washingtonpost.com/politics/edward-snowden-says-motive-behind-leaks-was-to-expose-surveillance-state/2013/06/09/aa3f0804-d13b-11e2-a73e-826d299ff459_story.html?wprss=rss_politics.

---

[156] Jason Howerton, "NSA Chief Denies Key Claim Made by PRISM Whistleblower, Claims Spying Has Disrupted Dozens of Terror Attacks," *The Blaze,* June 12, 2013, http://www.theblaze.com/stories/2013/06/12/nsa-chief-denies-key-claim-made-by-prism-whistleblower-claims-spying-has-disrupted-dozens-of-terror-attacks/.

[157] Chloe Albanesius, "Microsoft Joins Google, Asks to Reveal Secret FISA Data, *PC Magazine,* June 27, 2013, http://www.pcmag.com/article2/0,2817,2421078,00.asp.

[158] NATO, CCDCOE, "Our Mission & Vision," https://ccdcoe.org/structure-0.html.

[159] MG Siegler, "Eric Schmidt: Every 2 Days We Create as Much Information as We Did Up To 2003," *Tech Crunch,* August 4, 2010, http://techcrunch.com/2010/08/04/schmidt-data/.

[160] James Bamford, "The NSA Is Building the Country's Biggest Spy Center (Watch What You Say)," *Wired,* March 3, 2012, http://www.wired.com/2012/03/ff_nsadatacenter/.

[161] Amy Zegart and Marshall Erwin, "The NSA's image problem," *Los Angeles Times,* November 1, 2013, http://articles.latimes.com/2013/nov/01/opinion/la-oe-zegart-nsa-effectiveness-20131101.

[162] Susan Crabtree, "NSA chief: Press exaggerating spying to sell papers," *Washington Examiner,* October 30, 2013, http://www.washingtonexaminer.com/nsa-chief-press-exaggerating-spying-to-sell-papers/article/2538223.

[163] Crabtree, http://articles.latimes.com/2013/nov/01/opinion/la-oe-zegart-nsa-effectiveness-2013110.

[164] NPR, "Shadow Brokers Group Leaks Stolen National Security Agency Hacking Tools," *All Things Considered* (June 20, 2017), https://www.npr.org/2017/06/29/534916031/shadow-brokers-group-leaks-stolen-national-security-agency-hacking-tools. A very useful timeline (with sources) of the leaks is found in Wikipedia, "The Shadow Brokers," https://en.wikipedia.org/wiki/The_Shadow_Brokers.

Chapter 5

[165] Adam Entous, Ellen Nakashima, and Greg Miller, "Secret CIA assessment says Russia was trying to help Trum win White House," *Washington Post* (December 9, 2016), https://www.washingtonpost.com/world/national-security/obama-orders-review-of-russian-hacking-during-presidential-campaign/2016/12/09/31d6b300-be2a-11e6-94ac-3d324840106c_story.html?utm_term=.c833c17f272a.

[166] Alex Johnson, "WikiLeaks' Julian Assange: 'No Proof' Hacked DNC Emails Came From Russia," NBC News (July 25, 2016) and Diona Chiacu, "Moscow denies Russian involvement in U.S. DNC hacking," Reuters (June 14, 2016), http://www.reuters.com/article/us-usa-election-hack-russia-idUSKCN0Z02EK.

167 Eric Lipton and Scott Shane, "Democratic House Candidates Were Also Targets of Russian Hacking," *New York Times* (December 13, 2016), http://nyti.ms/2hCOgEY; David E. Sanger, Scott Shane, *New York Times,* "Russia hacked Republican committee but kept data, U.S. concludes," *Houston Chronicle* (December 9, 2016).

168 Adam Entous and Ellen Nakishima, "FBI backs CIA view that Russia intervened to help Trump win election," *Washington Post* (December 16, 2016), https://www.washingtonpost.com/world/national-security/fbi-backs-cia-view-that-russia-intervened-to-help-trump-win-election/2016/12/16/05b42c0e-c3bf-11e6-9a51-cd56ea1c2bb7_story.html?hpid=hp_hp-top-table-main_usrussia-224pm%3Ahomepage%2Fstory&utm_term=.4cb2778c3e66.

169 Christi Parsons and Brian Bennett, "Obama says election cyberattack came from the 'highest levels' of the Russian government and vows retaliation," *Los Angeles Times* (December 16, 2016), http://www.latimes.com/politics/la-na-pol-obama-end-of-year-news-conference-20161216-story.html.

170 Amy Chozick, "Clinton Says 'Personal Beef' by Putin Led to Hacking Attacks," *New York Times* (December 16, 2016), http://www.nytimes.com/2016/12/16/us/politics/hillary-clinton-russia-fbi-comey.html.

171 Stephen Collinson and Elise Labott, "Donald Trump takes aim at US intelligence community on Russia," CNN Politics, http://www.cnn.com/2016/12/10/politics/donald-trump-response-russian-hacking/; Rebecca Savransky, "Trump: 'Ridiculous' to think Russia intervened in election," *The Hill* (December 11, 2016), http://thehill.com/homenews/campaign/309839-trump-on-cia-assessment-i-think-its-ridiculous.

172 Bryan Schatz, "A History of Donald Trump's Bromance with Vladimir Putin," *Mother Jones* (October 5, 2016), http://www.motherjones.com/politics/2016/10/trump-putin-timeline.

173 Devlin Barrett and Philip Rucker, "Trump said he was thinking of Russia controversy when he decided to fire Comey," *Washington Post* (May 11, 2017), https://www.washingtonpost.com/world/national-security/trump-says-fbi-director-comey-told-him-three-times-he-wasnt-under-investigation-once-in-a-phone-call-initiated-by-the-president/2017/05/11/2b384c9a-3669-11e7-b4ee-434b6d506b37_story.html?utm_term=.a5d0ef6330c0.

174 Eric Lipton, David E. Sanger, and Scott Shane, "The Perfect Weapon: How Russian Cyberpower Invaded the U.S.," *New York Times* (December 13, 2016), http://www.nytimes.com/2016/12/13/us/politics/russia-hack-election-dnc.html.

175 Sarwar A. Kashmeri, *NATO 2.0: Reboot or Delete?* (Washington, D.C.: Potomac Books, 2011), 51.

176 David Albright, Paul Brannan, and Christina Walrond, "Did Stuxnet Take Out 1,000 Centrifuges at the Natanz Enrichment Plant?" Institute for Science and International Security ISIS Report, http://isis-online.org/uploads/isis-reports/documents/stuxnet_FEP_22Dec2010.pdf.

177 Anthony Fainberg, "Osirak and international security," *The Bulletin of the Atomic Scientists* (October 1981), 33-36, https://books.google.com/books?id=PQsAAAAAMBAJ&pg=PA33&dq=nuclear+fuel+osirak&hl=sv&ei=tK_0TKaPFY7oOdP-iKsI&sa=X&oi=book_result&ct=result&resnum=1&ved=0CCkQ6AEwAA#v=onepage&q=nuclear%20fuel%20osirak&f=false.

178 Benjamin Mueller, "Why we need a cyberwar treaty," *The Guardian* (June 2, 2014), https://www.theguardian.com/commentisfree/2014/jun/02/we-need-cyberwar-treaty; Joseph S. Nye Jr., "The world needs new norms on cyberwarfare," *Washington Post* (October 1, 2015), https://www.washingtonpost.com/opinions/the-world-needs-an-arms-control-treaty-for-cybersecurity/2015/10/01/20c3e970-66dd-11e5-9223-70cb36460919_story.html?utm_term=.bb5abea2b1a1.

179 Staff, "The COE International Convention on Cybercrime Before its Entry into Force," *Copyright Bulletin* (January-March 2004), http://portal.unesco.org/culture/en/ev.php-URL_ID=19556&URL_DO=DO_TOPIC&URL_SECTION=201.html; Council of Europe, "Chart of signatures and ratifications of Treaty 185," http://www.coe.int/en/web/conventions/full-list/-/conventions/treaty/185/signatures.

180 Council of Europe, "Convention on Cybercrime," Preamble, opened for signature November 23, 2001, C.E.T.S. No. 185.

181 Jack Goldsmith, "Cybersecurity Treaties: A Skeptical View," Hoover Institution (2011), 3, http://media.hoover.org/sites/default/files/documents/FutureChallenges_Goldsmith.pdf.

182 Goldsmith, 3-4.

183 Pete Kasperowicz, "House approves resolution to keep Internet control out of UN hands," *The Hill* (December 5, 2012), http://thehill.com/blogs/floor-action/house/271153-house-approves-resolution-to-keep-internet-control-out-of-un-hands.

184 ITU website, http://www.itu.int/en/Pages/default.aspx.

185 The discussion that follows is based on my own privately circulated but unpublished whitepaper of 2012, "NATO in Cyberspace: Creating a Future for the Greatest Alliance in Modern History."

186 NATO Summit, NATO Press Release, "The Alliance's Strategic Concept," April 24, 1999, http://www.internationaldemocracywatch.org/attachments/344_Nato%20Strategic%20Concept%20(1999).pdf.

187 Qiao Liang and Wang Xiangsui, *Unrestricted Warfare* (1999; New Delhi: Natraj, 2007), 9.

188 Qiao Liang and Wang Xiangsui, 16-17.

189 Qiao Liang and Wang Xiangsui, 33-34.

190 NATO, "Defending Against Cyber Attacks,"
http://www.nato.int/cps/en/natolive/topics_49193.htm.
191 Sarwar A. Kashmeri, *NATO 2.0: Reboot or Delete?* (Washington, D.C.:
Potomac Books, 2011), 53; NATO Watch, "Call for NATO running costs to be
made public on 'International Right to Know Day' 10th Anniversary,"
September 28, 2012, http://www.natowatch.org/node/769; CCDCOE, "Mission
and Vision," https://www.ccdcoe.org/11.html.
192 The North Atlantic Treaty, April 4, 1949.
193 CCDCOE, "Publications," https://www.ccdcoe.org/4.html.
194 CCDCOE, "Exercises & Courses," https://www.ccdcoe.org/6.html.
195 CCDCOE, "Exercises & Courses," https://www.ccdcoe.org/6.html.
196 CCDCOE, Tallinn Manual, https://ccdcoe.org/tallinn-manual.html.
197 NATO, "Chicago Summit Declaration," May 20, 2012,
http://www.nato.int/cps/en/natolive/official_texts_87593.htm?selectedLo
cale=en.
198 NATO, "Chicago Summit Declaration"; NATO, "NATO and cyber defence,"
http://www.nato.int/cps/en/SID-ECD47F01-
D91E3955/natolive/topics_78170.htm?
199 Häly Laasme, "Estonia: Cyber Window into the Future of NATO," *JFQ* (4th
quarter 2011), issue 63, 60, http://www.ndu.edu/press/lib/images/jfq-
63/JFQ63_58-63_Laasme.pdf.
200 Laasme, 60.
201 Zbigniew Brzezinski, "An Agenda for NATO: Toward a Global Security
Web," *Foreign Affairs,* September/October 2009,
http://www.foreignaffairs.com/articles/65240/zbigniew-brzezinski/an-agenda-
for-nato.
202 Ibid.
203 CCDE, "NATO Centres of Excellence," https://ccdcoe.org/nato-centres-
excellence.html.
204 David Z. Morris, "Trump Cybersecurity Advisors Resign, Citing His
'Insufficient Attention' to Threats," *Fortune* (August 26, 2017),
http://fortune.com/2017/08/26/trump-cybersecurity-advisors-resign/.
205 Ryan Browne, "[U.S. Secretary of Defense James] Mattis: U.S. South Korea
cooperation urgent in face of 'accelerated' North Korea threat," CNN Politics
(October 29, 2017), http://www.cnn.com/2017/10/28/politics/mattis-north-
korea-nuclear-threat/index.html.
206 David E. Sanger, David D. Kirkpatrick, and Nicole Perlroth, "The World
Once Laughed at North Korean Cyberpower. No More," *New York Times*
(October 15, 2017), https://www.nytimes.com/2017/10/15/world/asia/north-
korea-hacking-cyber-sony.html?_r=0.
207 Choe Sang-Hun and Gerry Mullany, "North Korea in 'state of war' as fresh
cyberattack claims emerge," *The Globe and Mail,* March 31, 2013,
http://www.theglobeandmail.com/news/world/north-korea-in-state-of-war-as-

fresh-cyberattack-claims-emerge/article10586425/; Richard A. Clarke and Robert K. Knake, *Cyber War: THe Next Threat to National Security and What to Do About It* (New York: HarperCollins, 2010), 24-26.
[208] Clarke, 23.

Chapter 6

[209] Central Intelligence Agency, *The World Factbook,* https://www.cia.gov/library/publications/the-world-factbook/geos/us.html.
[210] Greg Miller, "Undersea Internet Cables Are Surprisingly Vulnerable," *Wired* (October 29, 2015), https://www.wired.com/2015/10/undersea-cable-maps/.
[211] Matthew Carle, "Operation Ivy Bells," *Military.com Remembers the Cold War,* http://www.military.com/Content/MoreContent1/?file=cw_f_ivybells. Pelton was tried, convicted, and sentenced to life imprisonment for his espionage.
[212] Tom Simonite, "The Seemingly Unfixable Crack in the Internet's Backbone," *MIT Technology Review* (August 6, 2015), https://www.technologyreview.com/s/540056/the-seemingly-unfixable-crack-in-the-internets-backbone/.
[213] Simonite, https://www.technologyreview.com/s/540056/the-seemingly-unfixable-crack-in-the-internets-backbone/.
[214] Lucas, Joe, and McManus, https://www.technologyreview.com/s/540056/the-seemingly-unfixable-crack-in-the-internets-backbone/.
[215] David E. Sanger and Eric Schmitt, "Russian Ships Near Data Cables Are Too Close for U.S. Comfort," *New York Times* (October 25, 2015), http://www.nytimes.com/2015/10/26/world/europe/russian-presence-near-undersea-cables-concerns-us.html?_r=0.
[216] Glenn Greenwald, "NSA Prism program taps in to user data of Apple, Google and others," *The Guardian* (June 7, 2013), https://www.theguardian.com/world/2013/jun/06/us-tech-giants-nsa-data; Barton Gellman and Laura Poitras, "U.S., British intelligence mining data from nine U.S. Internet companies in broad secret program," *Washington Post* (June 7, 2013), https://www.washingtonpost.com/investigations/us-intelligence-mining-data-from-nine-us-internet-companies-in-broad-secret-program/2013/06/06/3a0c0da8-cebf-11e2-8845-d970ccb04497_story.html?utm_term=.b6f45edcf604.
[217] http://www.nytimes.com/2005/02/20/politics/new-nuclear-sub-is-said-to-have-special-eavesdropping-ability.html
[218] Fabian Schmidt, "Tapping the world's fiber optic cables," Deutsche Welle (June 30, 2013), http://www.dw.com/en/tapping-the-worlds-fiber-optic-cables/a-16916476.
[219] http://www.theatlantic.com/international/archive/2013/07/the-creepy-long-standing-practice-of-undersea-cable-tapping/277855/

[220] Charles Sumner, *The Works of Charles Sumner* (Boston: Lee and Shepard, 1875), 3:507. Also see, Raymond Koehler, "Ray Koehler on 'Fiat Iustitia Ruat Caelum" (February 13, 2012), http://koehlerlaw.net/2012/02/ray-koehler-on-fiat-iustitia-ruat-caelum/.

[221] The following material has been developed from J.R. Smith and Siobhan MacDermott, *Wide Open Privacy: Strategies for the Digital Life* (Birmingham, MI: IT-Harvest Press, 2012), chapter 8.

[222] Andrew Marvell, "To His Coy Mistress," Poetry Foundation, https://www.poetryfoundation.org/poems-and-poets/poems/detail/44688.

[223] "These were the biggest hacks, leaks and data breaches of 2016," ZDNet (November 15, 2016), http://www.zdnet.com/pictures/biggest-hacks-security-data-breaches-2016/ and "2017's biggest hacks, leaks, and data breaches—so far," ZDNet (September 20, 2017), http://www.zdnet.com/pictures/biggest-hacks-leaks-and-data-breaches-2017/.

[224] Steve Morgan, "Cyber Crime Costs Projected to Reach #2 Trillion by 2019," *Forbes* (January 17, 2016), http://www.forbes.com/sites/stevemorgan/2016/01/17/cyber-crime-costs-projected-to-reach-2-trillion-by-2019/#a7262f23bb0c; Juniper Research, "Cybercrime Will Cost Businesses Over $2 Trillion by 2019" (May 12m 2015), https://www.juniperresearch.com/press/press-releases/cybercrime-cost-businesses-over-2trillion.

[225] Matthew 7:24-27 and Luke 6:46-49.

[226] The discussion that follows draws on Siobhan MacDermott and J. R. Smith, *Cybermilitia: A Citizen Strategy to Fight, Win, and War in Cyberspace* (Birmingham, MI: IT-Harvest Press, 2013).

[227] Eric Engleman, "Cybersecurity Bill Killed, Paving Way for Executive Order," *Bloomberg,* November 4, 2012, http://www.bloomberg.com/news/2012-11-15/cybersecurity-bill-killed-paving-way-for-executive-order.html.

[228] Barack Obama, "Executive Order—Improving Critical Infrastructure Cybersecurity," February 12, 2013, http://m.whitehouse.gov/the-press-office/2013/02/12/executive-order-improving-critical-infrastructure-cybersecurity.

[229] See, for example, Brian Prince, "Obama Cybersecurity Executive Order A First Step, But More Is Needed, Some Say," *Security Dark Reading*, February 13, 2013, http://www.darkreading.com/compliance/167901112/security/news/240148564/obama-cyber-security-executive-order-a-first-step-but-more-is-needed-some-say.html, and Chenxi Wang, "Obama's Cybersecurity Executive Order: Heart In The Right Place But There Is Little Teeth," *Forbes,* February 14, 2013, http://www.forbes.com/sites/forrester/2013/02/14/obamas-cybersecurity-executive-order-heart-in-the-right-place-but-there-is-little-teeth/.

[230] Obama, Executive Order, Sec. 10.

[231] *District of Columbia v. Heller*—07-290 (2008), http://supreme.justia.com/cases/federal/us/554/07-290/.

---

[232] "An Act To promote the efficiency of the militia, and for other purposes," http://legisworks.org/sal/32/stats/STATUTE-32-Pg775.pdf.
[233] "What Is the Militia," http://www.lawandliberty.org/what_mil.htm.
[234] Legal Information Institute, "U.S. Code § 246 – Militia: composition and classes," https://www.law.cornell.edu/uscode/text/10/246.
[235] Alexander Klimberg quoted in Jeffrey Carr, *Inside Cyber Warfare* (N.p.: O'Reilly Media, 2011), Kindle Edition, chap. 13.
[236] Carr, Preface.

www.ingramcontent.com/pod-product-compliance
Lightning Source LLC
Chambersburg PA
CBHW051746250726
48659CB00001B/273